ABORIGINAL PEOPLE AND COLONIZERS OF WESTERN CANADA TO 1900

D0887638

The history of Canada's Aboriginal peoples after European contact is a hotly debated area of study. In *Aboriginal People and Colonizers of Western Canada to 1900*, Sarah Carter looks at the cultural, political, and economic issues of this contested history, focusing on the Western interior, or what would later become Canada's Prairie provinces.

This wide-ranging survey draws on the wealth of interdisciplinary scholarship of the last three decades. Topics include the impact of European diseases, changing interpretations of fur trade interaction, the Red River settlement as a cultural crossroad, missionaries, treaties, the disappearance of the buffalo, the myths about the Mounties, Canadian 'Indian' policy, and the policies of Aboriginal peoples towards Canada.

Carter focuses on the multiplicity of perspectives that exist on past events. Referring to nearly all of the current scholarship in the field, she presents opposing versions on every major topic, often linking these debates to contemporary issues. The result is a sensitive treatment of history as an interpretive exercise, making this an invaluable text for students as well as all those interested in Aboriginal/non-Aboriginal relations.

(Themes in Canadian Social History)

SARAH CARTER is a professor in the Department of History at the University of Calgary.

THEMES IN CANADIAN SOCIAL HISTORY

Editor: Craig Heron

SARAH CARTER

Aboriginal People
and Colonizers
of Western Canada to 1900

UNIVERSITY OF TORONTO PRESS
Toronto Buffalo London

© University of Toronto Press Incorporated 1999
Toronto Buffalo London

Printed in Canada
Reprinted 2007, 2010

ISBN 0-8020-4147-7 (cloth)
ISBN 0-8020-7995-4 (paper)

Printed on acid-free paper

Canadian Cataloguing in Publication Data

Carter, Sarah, 1954–
    Aboriginal people and colonizers of Western Canada to 1900

    (Themes in Canadian social history)
    Includes bibliographical references and index.
    ISBN 0-8020-4147-7 (bound)   ISBN 0-8020-7995-4 (pbk.)

    1. Northwest, Canadian – Ethnic relations.   2. Indians of
North America – Prairie Provinces – History.   3. Métis –
Prairie Provinces – History.*   4. Northwest, Canadian –
History – To 1870.*   5. Northwest, Canadian – History –
1870–1905.* 6. Indians of North America – Prairie Provinces –
First contact with Europeans.   I. Title. II. Series.

    E78.P7C377 1999   971.2'00497   C99-931368-1

University of Toronto Press acknowledges the financial
assistance to its publishing program of the Canada Council for
the Arts and the Ontario Arts Council.

University of Toronto Press acknowledges the financial support for its publishing activities of the Government of Canada
through the Book Publishing Industry Development Program
(BPIDP).

Canada

To the memory of Irene M. Spry
Professor Emeritus, Department of Economics
University of Ottawa

Contents

Acknowledgments

I am grateful to the Department of Archaeology of the University of Calgary, and especially to Dr Jane H. Kelley and Dr Nick David, for providing me with congenial writing space during the term of my Killam Resident Fellowship, which permitted me to complete work on this book. I would like to thank the Killam Foundation for this award. I also appreciated the superb editorial assistance and guidance of Dr Craig Heron, and I thank the University of Toronto Press for the invitation to write this book. The comments of an anonymous reviewer were very helpful. Colleagues and students at the universities of Saskatchewan, Manitoba, Winnipeg, and Calgary have contributed a great deal to the contents of this book. Thanks to Harold Cardinal for providing me with a copy of his LLM thesis from Harvard Law School, and for his insights into Cree history and world-view. Thanks are also due to Rick Lalonde of Calgary, who drew the map. I am grateful to University of Calgary history honours students Robert Bridge, Jennifer Howse, and Kathleen Renne for their helpful comments on the final draft of this work.

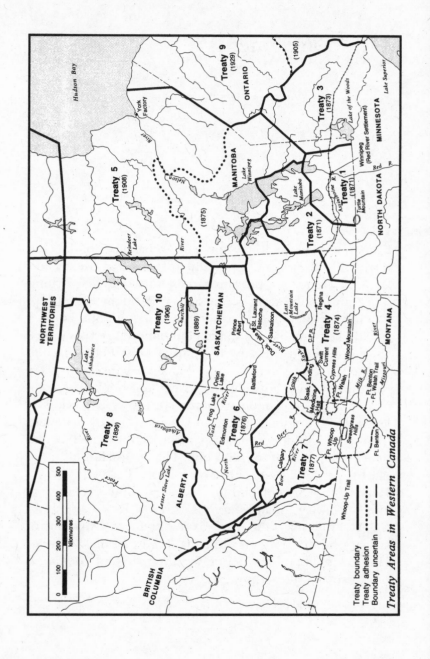

Treaty Areas in Western Canada

ABORIGINAL PEOPLE AND COLONIZERS OF WESTERN CANADA TO 1900

Introduction

The area around the village of Herschel, in west-central Saskatchewan, is a rich source of ancient Aboriginal artefacts, including tipi rings, cairns, firepits, rock alignments, buffalo jumps, kill and processing sites, a medicine wheel, and ceremonial and vision-quest sites. There are also petroglyphs (images carved on rocks). The largest and most remarkable of these stones has the appearance of a recumbent buffalo, and part of it has been systematically carved and grooved to resemble the animal's ribcage. Like other ancient artefacts of the world, such as Stonehenge, this ribstone petroglyph has generated many theories about its uses and meaning. It may have had astronomical significance, as the rock is precisely positioned to face the east and to show the equinox. It was likely a sacred site, as there is evidence of cultural offerings at the base of the rock. It may have been a teaching stone, carved to represent the First Peoples' understanding of the life journey and of the buffalo as the source of life. But what the ribstone petroglyph and the other artefacts clearly attest to is the great antiquity of the civilizations that have occupied Western Canada. A buffalo horn found at a processing site is 2,065 years old, and carbon-dating puts the earliest finds at A.D. 350. Clearly, a remarkably stable and highly successful way of life persisted for thousands of years.

Generations of Aboriginal people found the Eagle and Bear Hills near Herschel to be an ideal location, as the area had buffalo, shelter, water, wildfowl, berries, and plenty of trees. Beginning about 100 years ago, newly arrived immigrants to Western Canada hoped that these hills could be their ideal habitat. Around 1910 my grandfather, from a small village near London, England, was among the hopefuls who attempted to homestead in the Eagle Hills. Although he came armed with a book on how to build a house (and another on how to play the zither), this venture lasted only briefly, as it did for a great number of the would-be homesteaders who were unprepared for survival on the Northern Plains. Others were more successful: a new farming society and economy was established, and at times prospered. Most of the newcomers to Western Canada were confident that a superior way of life was supplanting an Aboriginal past that had nothing to teach them. Although in 1772–3 Hudson's Bay Company employee Matthew Cocking observed the stone cairns, tipi rings, pottery, and other archaeological treasures of the Eagle Hills, later generations of European visitors ignored, then forgot, them. Today, at a time when the new agricultural economy is not flourishing, residents of Herschel see the key to the survival and future of their community in the Aboriginal past and the ancient treasures that they hope will attract visitors and provide a new lease on life. Although named for an English astronomer, the town of Herschel will depict Aboriginal astronomy, among other themes, in the deserted schoolhouse that will serve as the interpretive centre. Herschel is not alone in this venture, as other prairie locations, small and large, have set about to capitalize on this unique heritage as a means of revitalizing communities.

These developments demonstrate a shift in non-Aboriginal attitudes and interests. Just thirty years ago, students at Canadian universities were told that there was not any Aboriginal history to teach, and no history courses were offered that dealt in a substantive way with the topic of Aboriginal and European contact. At that time, there would have been very few books and articles upon which to base a course, or even part of a course. The history texts then available provided very little insight into Canada's First Nations. In his 1947 text, which was still assigned reading in introductory history courses well into the 1970s, University of Toronto history professor Edgar McInnis hastily dismissed the topic with these words: 'The Europeans who came to the shores of North America regarded it as a vacant continent, which lay completely open to settlement from the Old World. In the final analysis this assumption was justified ... The aborigines made no major contribution to the culture that developed in the settled communities of Canada ... They remained a primitive remnant clinging to their tribal organization long after it had become obsolete.'

Much has changed since that time. Many courses and vast numbers of books, articles, theses, and reports now fill the silences and challenge the old prejudices. This dramatic outpouring and transformation of the field may in part be explained by the influence of what has been known since the 1980s as 'post-colonialism.' Spokespersons of cultures once subjected to European colonization have criticized the way history became a form of writing that is dominated and controlled by the 'winners,' that assumed the superiority of white culture and its civilizing mission, and that discounted, ignored, or misunderstood indigenous cultures.

In North America, the 1992 Columbus Quincentennial helped draw attention to compelling questions about how history has been written and exhibited – whose voices have been included and whose have been left out. Although these questions had been raised decades before, in 1992 they began to receive widespread attention. In Canada, Aboriginal scholars, politicians, social activists, artists, writers, and teachers succeeded in moving an awareness of

Aboriginal issues closer to the centre stage of Canadian consciousness. So did important legal challenges, such as the 1973 *Calder* case, that paved the way for the recognition of Aboriginal rights in the 1982 Canadian Constitution Act.

The tremendous surge of studies in the field of Aboriginal and culture contact history also has to do with the interest in and respectability accorded to what has been broadly termed 'social history,' the study of ordinary women and men, from working-class backgrounds and from ethnic/racial minorities. Writing Aboriginal history posed particular challenges. The records documenting Aboriginal/European relations from the seventeenth to the early twentieth century were produced overwhelmingly by one side of this relationship alone – fur traders, explorers, missionaries, then government officials, the North-West Mounted Police Forces, and assorted immigrants. The vast majority of these predominantly male observers present a distorted and narrow view of Aboriginal societies. Many had limited understanding of the cultures and languages of the people they encountered, and they were confident in the superiority of their cultures, values, religions, achievements, and lifeways. These European descriptions remain important to the historian, but they must be used with caution. By drawing upon the insights of anthropologists and archaeologists, and in other ways learning about and from Aboriginal people, historians more recently have attempted to gain some understanding of the lifeways of Aboriginal as well as European societies in order to evaluate and interpret the documentary record, recognizing the biases and preconceptions. Some of the scholars who combine anthropological models with historical methods and documentary sources call themselves 'ethnohistorians.'

Many draw on non-documentary forms of evidence, artefacts, and other material remains. Aboriginal societies left more records, or documents, than earlier generations of non-Aboriginal historians were prepared to recognize. Winter counts, for example, of Northern Plains people are chronologies comprising lists of names, or titles for each year, recording the most significant event for that year, which is represented by pictographs. Calendar sticks with marks and symbols, like the pictographs of winter counts, served to jog the memory of the oral historian. There are also rock paintings, rock effigies, birchbark migration charts, and carvings. Drawings on shirts, robes, tipi covers, and shields portray past events and exploits. The past was also preserved through symbolic regalia and expressive performances, as during the ceremonies of the Ojibway Midewiwin (healing medicine society). Prayers and songs record historical journeys, and origin-migration history. By the late nineteenth century, many autobiographies were being written with the assistance of non-Aboriginal collaborators. In Western Canada, Red Crow of the Bloods and Eagle Ribs of the Tsuu T'ina had their autobiographies recorded.

Aboriginal peoples primarily used oral narratives to preserve and convey their own past. There are sacred narratives involving non-human characters, and more factual, often historical narratives featuring human characters. There are also fictional, entertaining, and often humorous stories, involving the interplay of humans and non-humans. Academic historians have been slow to recognize any of these as legitimate sources. There is concern that oral sources are prone to be shaped and altered by the storyteller's present-day purposes, and that it is impossible to sift through to the 'facts.' However, this attitude is becoming less prevalent. The rich oral literature of Aboriginal peoples can no longer be dismissed as something 'quaint,' but not reliable, if we hope to come to a multidimensional understanding of cultures in contact. It is clear that the intent of much storytelling in oral societies is not to convey accurate information about the past, but some accounts are intended for this purpose. In Cree narratives, there is a basic distinction between the *acimowin*, the factual account, and the *kakeskihkemowin*, or counselling text.

Speakers carefully distinguish between what they experienced themselves, and what had been told to them by others. All historians choose their topics, and the way in which they interpret and present them, in the light of their own predilections and interests. All sources, whether oral, documentary, or material, must be read critically, rather than literally. Some representations of the past found in both oral and archival sources may be far from reliable.

In the last three decades, historians have made great efforts to present Aboriginal people as genuine participants, and to have sensitivity to the perspective of Aboriginal people as well as that of the Europeans. Yet concerns and criticisms remain that a partial and distorted view of the past is being perpetuated. The vast majority of the scholars whose work is presented in this book are themselves non-Aboriginal, and most of them remain reliant for their sources upon admittedly problematic documents. Some critics have gone so far as to suggest that people who are not of Aboriginal ancestry cannot comprehend the world-views of Aboriginal people of the past, and therefore are not capable of writing about them. The historical orientations and world-views of Aboriginal and Western societies are perceived by some to be fundamentally opposite. Reflecting on her experience of preparing a film series that would depict the history of Canada from an Aboriginal point of view, Métis film-maker Christine Welsh wrote that 'looking at history from the native perspective meant much more than seeing historical events from a different point of view. It meant surrendering our pre-conceived notions of the very nature of history – that it is linear, progressive, date- and event-oriented – and adapting our thinking to a fundamentally different aboriginal world-view which is cyclical and ultimately timeless.'

This book provides a general outline and understanding of the history of Aboriginal people and Europeans in contact in the territory that was to become the three 'Prairie' provinces of Canada. It is based on the wealth of historical scholarship produced in the last three decades. It will highlight some of the new approaches and interpretations, often conflicting, that have emerged, showing the strengths of the recent literature, but it will also suffer from the limitations of the literature, including the continued heavy reliance on traditional historical methods and sources. The work of these scholars indicates the degree to which Aboriginal history cannot be separated from Canadian history; people were interconnected then, as they are today. A major purpose of the book is to point out that, to understand issues of vital concern to Canadians today, it is necessary to have knowledge of the past and to appreciate that there are often conflicting interpretations of the past, sometimes clearly as a result of present-day concerns. Lively and intense debates about the past are very often linked to issues that are before the courts and Indian claims commissions today, and that are discussed in Parliament and in the press, as well as at academic conferences.

The book introduces students to two central debates in early Western Canadian history. The first focuses on the question of human agency. The great majority of the scholars represented here have attempted to dramatically shift and expand the focus of historical inquiry from Europeans to Aboriginal people. They are reacting against earlier approaches that saw a weak and subordinate people quickly disappearing from sight. Most of the scholars whose work is presented here have stressed the power of human agency, drawing upon developments in other areas of social history, including women's, working-class, and ethnic history. Within this framework Aboriginal people are no longer cast as 'passive victims' but as 'active agents,' genuine actors with strategies and interests of their own that they rigorously pursued. They had some control over their own fate, despite the uneven power relationship that eventually favoured Europeans. As active agents they did not allow themselves to be victimized. The history of contact, then, is no longer seen as one dominant group imposing will and authority on an oppressed group; rather, it is seen as a process of reciprocity and exchange among all participants. Such an approach was evident first in studies of the fur-trade era, and more recently it has emerged in studies of the era of treaties, missionaries, and reserves.

There is some debate about this interpretation. As two Canadian historians have recently asked, has the idea of Aboriginal agency become 'colonialist alibi'? Has 'evidence of Native resilience and strength [been used] to soften, and at times deny, the impact of colonialism, and thus, implicitly, to absolve its perpetrators?' Have scholars gone too far in stressing agency, and in the course of this have they overlooked or downplayed the resourcefulness, ingenuity, motives, initiatives, and strategies of the Euro-Canadian side?

Another debate about the history of Aboriginal/European contact has focused upon the issue of what motivated the behaviour of Aboriginal people of the past. There are conflicting interpretations that Bruce Trigger has identified as 'romantic versus rationalistic.' The romantics, or cultural relativists, accord 'to the beliefs transmitted within specific cultures a preeminent role as determinants of human behavior.' The economic behaviour of Aboriginal people during the era of the European fur trade is understood to have been deeply embedded in beliefs and traditions that shaped perceptions and values. European goods were valued, not for their utilitarian properties, but for their religious or symbolic significance, and Aboriginal people entered into trade with Europeans on the basis of traditional evaluations, and therefore for different reasons than their trade partners – that is, not to make a profit, but to cement alliances and to enhance prestige. The Aboriginals' motives were not profit-driven and market-oriented; they had an internal logic of behaviour and motivation that was distinct from that of Europeans. Non-economic purposes shaped the exchange of goods, with gifts signifying rank and prestige playing an important part, as they did in diplomacy and intertribal trade. Those on this side of the debate stress that Aboriginal groups were little influenced by European technology. They emphasize the continuity rather than the disintegration of Aboriginal cultural traditions and identities, downplaying the impact of the fur trade. Aboriginal culture and society were not as fragile as a house of cards. There was cultural exchange, a reciprocal process in which both Aboriginal and European underwent change. Those on this side of the debate also tend to stress that there was a tremendous diversity of encounters between Aboriginal and European, and that any generalizations about colonialism and its consequences are likely to be invalid. We must examine specific locales, specific cultures, at specific times.

On the other side of the debate are the rationalists, who claim that human behaviour is shaped by calculations of individual self-interest that are uniform from one culture to another. According to Trigger the rationalistic philosophy 'stresses the universality of human nature and maintains that through the exercise of reason human groups at the same general level of development will respond in a similar way to the same kinds of challenges.' In this view, in their economic interactions with Europeans in the fur trade, Aboriginal traders and hunters based their decisions upon material, utilitarian, and not spiritual considerations. Reason, calculation, and choice could cause even the most cherished beliefs to be discarded. The rationalists tend to emphasize a growing reliance upon Europeans, and the impact this contact had on Aboriginal societies and economies.

Not all scholars readily or tidily fit into one or the other camp; most acknowledge persuasive arguments on both sides, and some seek to reconcile the two positions. Bruce Trigger has argued that no scholar in this field can overlook the importance of cultural traditions in influencing behaviour. He contends that detailed knowedge of Aboriginal cultures is vital, but he cautions against the faulty assumption that these traditions are static, surviving unaltered through hundreds of years. He stresses that people change, as their circumstances and environment change. With regard to the lengthy course of fur-trade history, Trigger argues that cultural beliefs may have significantly influenced Aboriginal reactions in the early stages of their encounters with Europeans, but as relations became more direct and intense, rationalist calculations came to play a preponderant role. They were not constrained by traditional beliefs; rather, they made a rational assessment of the dangers and opportunities. Trigger concludes that in the long run a rationalist analysis of cultural interaction seems to explain far more about what happened to Aboriginal people after contact (although he notes that the romantic approach has acquired enormous influence in the last two decades). Those on the rationalist side of the debate are more prone to see some basic patterns to the relations between Europeans and indigenous peoples in the course of the expansion of the European world system. As Trigger has written, 'Had relations between Europeans and native peoples been determined mainly by their respective ideologies, much more variation could be expected.'

My own research that focuses on the post-treaty era suggests that Aboriginal people of the Plains of Western Canada were not constrained by traditional cultural beliefs, as other scholars have contended. Religious and cultural beliefs did not prevent them from seeing that the buffalo, and thus the foundation of their economy, were disappearing and that steps had to be taken to create a new economic base – agriculture. That their initiatives eventually failed was not a product of cultural traditions that supposedly made them unsuited for a life of farming, although this idea was vigorously promoted by government administrators. At the same time, however, it is clear that Aboriginal people saw no need to divest themselves of culture, institutions, and arrangements such as their sacred ceremonies and religious beliefs. There was persistence and continuity in the face of the rapid changes.

A final theme that emerges several times in this book is that there were occasions in the past when it appeared that Aboriginal and non-Aboriginal in Western Canada might be able to establish progressive partnerships, to share in the land, resources, and economy. The legal framework for such a partnership was established in Western Canada in the 1870s through the Manitoba Act, and the treaties. I chose to end the book about 1900 as I believe it was then that any hope of partnership for the twentieth century was finally laid to rest. The year 1896 saw a change in the federal government from the Conservatives to the Wilfrid Laurier Liberals, but this was not of particular significance to the West, as there was continuity and persistence in policy. However, the change in government coincided with a new age of prosperity for Western Canada: the end of a drought cycle, a wheat boom, a great land rush. It was clear by this time that Aboriginal Westerners were not going to share in this prosperity, that paths had diverged. Ending at this point, the book is admittedly and regrettably a fairly gloomy story which challenges the dominant plotting of Western Canadian history as the chronicle of a place that became happier, richer, and better than it started out. Yet, the book has a positive goal: I hope it will serve to remind readers that Western Canada was intended to be common ground, in the hopes that it can genuinely become such a place in the near future. In a germinal article on this era in Western Canada, first published over twenty years ago, economic historian Irene Spry wrote about the 'tragedy' of the loss of the commons. This book is dedicated to Irene Spry, and her vision of a nation in which resources and wealth are equally shared.

A Note on Terminology

Throughout most of this book I have chosen to use the

term 'Aboriginal' as a replacement for the term 'Indian,' as
the latter is a historic blunder which began when Christo-
pher Columbus, landing in the Caribbean, believed that he
had reached India. I realize that 'Aboriginal' is problematic as well, however, especially as it erases the diversity of
very different peoples. Yet it is the term selected for use in
the Constitution Act 1982, and encompasses the Métis,
those defined as 'Indian' under the Indian Act, and those
not legally defined as 'Indians' (formerly known as 'non-
status Indians'). At times, however, particularly when
describing the late nineteenth century, I use 'Indian' when
it is necessary to distinguish those people whose lives were
administered pursuant to the Indian Act. I also use 'First
Nations' at times, to refer to those groups defined as 'Indians' by the Indian Act. (This term, however, is problematic
for other Aboriginal groups who feel the term implicitly
renders them 'Second Nations.') I capitalize the term
'Aboriginal.' As Paul Chartrand has pointed out, even the
term 'Highlanders' is capitalized when it refers to the people of the Scottish highlands, although the generic term
'highlander' is not capitalized when it refers to any inhab-
itant of any highland area. Whenever possible I shall refer
to the specific name of the people. Today, Aboriginal
nations are reclaiming their names for themselves, as often
names have been attached to them by others, sometimes by
Europeans and sometimes by other Aboriginal nations.
Some of these names have been the result of linguistic misunderstanding, and some are even offensive. The Tsuu
T'ina have reclaimed their own name recently, replacing
'Sarcee,' which was from a Blackfoot word meaning 'Bold
People.' The Siksika have also reclaimed their name,
replacing the English 'Blackfoot.'

1

Homeland

Origins of the First Peoples

Every community has creation stories that explain how the world came to be, how humans originated, and how their own particular group came to occupy their homeland. These stories are vital to the identity and cohesion of a community. They might incorporate moral teachings, and describe vital customs and laws. They often explain how people sharing a similar origin came to be distinct populations, and how they migrated from their point of origin. Creation stories reassure people that the place where they live was meant to be their home. The stories may contain acute observations of the environment, and of the behaviour of other forms of life.

The Aboriginal societies of the Americas identify this as their land of origin. The creation story of the Assiniboine of the Great Plains of northern North America focuses upon Ik-Tomi, the legendary character who created the world, and upon Lake Winnipeg, known to them as 'Holy Lake.' Ik-Tomi made the land, the waters, night, day, and heaven, and then he made seven women and seven men from the earth. He wanted to find the right place for them, so he gathered some large oyster shells, and upon these Ik-Tomi and the seven men and women floated. They paddled for many days, and, fearing they would all die from hunger and thirst, he called together all the waterfowl and selected seven from among them. They were to dive down to the bottom of the body of water and bring back some mud. The people waited for seven days and nights. On the seventh night the birds who had gone down began to float, dead, to the surface. Ik-Tomi found no mud on their tiny claws. He then selected the muskrat, mink, beaver, and fisher to dive down and bring back mud. All of these also returned dead, but Ik-Tomi found tiny specks of mud clinging to their paws. Carefully he took the mud from each and it was from this mud that he made the land that we are now on. He also made some large lakes, and at the edge of a lake he set his people. He made all things for them and taught them all they needed to know. According to Assiniboine legend, Lake Winnipeg was the great water where Ik-Tomi sent his people. To the Assiniboine, that lake represents the centre of the world; they believe they were created there.

Neither archaeologists, demographers, anthropologists nor geologists know, with any certainty, much about the origins of the First Peoples of the Americas, and there is by no means complete agreement among scholars. They have only fragments of evidence to work with. But scholars from these disciplines share the premise that *homo sapiens* did not evolve on this continent. No Neanderthal skeletal remains have been found in the western hemisphere. Human populations are believed to have spread from Africa over the earth's surface. Archaeologists and other scholars explain the peopling of the Americas as the result of migration from northeastern Asia across the Bering Strait via a land bridge (Beringia) that was exposed intermittently during the last ice age (14,000–20,000 years ago). There is now fairly widespread agreement that they might also have come by watercraft. Yet, a great deal of disagreement persists about when they came, how many waves of immigration there were, how long it took them to populate the Americas, and how the interior of the continent was populated. Scholars' estimates of the earliest date at which people may have arrived range from 30,000 to 100,000 years ago. Many scholars argue that people migrated through North America via one or more ice-free corridors, formed between two retreating ice masses, in particular one along the eastern ridge of today's Rocky Mountains. Others contest this theory entirely in favour of migration by water along the food-rich western coastline, arguing that immense continental and mountain glaciers would have ruled out movement through an ice-free corridor.

Scientific explanations of the origins of indigenous North Americans contradict, challenge, and ignore the ancient teachings of Aboriginal peoples. Native American scholar Vine Deloria Jr has called these explanations the 'origin myths' of Western science. Aboriginal people particularly object to the notion they were simply the first of many waves of immigrants. This issue is at the centre of claims for justice today as Aboriginal people attempt to persuade the courts that they have been here since 'time immemorial.' To immigrate is to come to a country of which one is not a native for the purpose of permanent settlement, and this is quite different from being recognized as aboriginal (belonging to a region from earliest times) or indigenous (belonging totally to), or autochthonous (aboriginal, indigenous).

Critics of the land-bridge and associated scientific theories also point out that science is not as objective and value-free as its practitioners allege. Theories about the arrival and dispersal of people through the continent, and estimates of population, vary greatly, and one variable is the very different notions scientists have had of the capabilities and skills of Aboriginal people to survive, cope, and adapt. It is only fair to say, however, that today a great number of scientists recognize the subjective and speculative nature of their theories. Deloria has called upon scientists to initiate more respectful discussions with elders, who can share some of their knowledge and wisdom. He believes that

Aboriginal people were 'here "at the beginning" and have preserved the memory of traumatic continental and planetary catastrophes, keeping the information sometimes in accounts deliberately constructed to preserve as well as entertain.'

Aboriginal people were here 'at the beginning,' unlike the many groups of immigrants who began to arrive much more recently. The sheer length of this tenure is difficult to conceive. The Aboriginal history gallery at the Provincial Museum of Alberta presents visitors immediately with the concept of 500 generations, or 11,000 years of residency. The author of a book on the Aboriginal people of the Great Lakes attempted to convey a sense of their immense tenure by having readers imagine that a home video covering all 12,000 years of human occupation lasted an entire year, running twenty-four hours a day, every day. According to that scale, each month would represent 1,000 years, and each day would represent about 33 years, or one generation. Viewers would see generations upon generations that would produce innovations and changes, and they would also see famines, battles, and human disasters. It would not be until 21 December that a French explorer would make a brief appearance. Only in the few remaining days of the year would non-Aboriginal people outnumber Aboriginal people, and modern farms and cities alter the landscape.

The Land

This book focuses upon the geographical area known today as the three 'Prairie provinces' – Manitoba, Saskatchewan, and Alberta – but for most of the time period under consideration here these provincial boundaries and the international boundary did not exist at all. The focus of the book will not always manage to stay strictly within these arbitrary confines, as they were not recognized by the people who originally occupied these lands, or by their European visitors and later residents. The term 'Prairie provinces' is itself a misnomer, as these encompass three main geographic zones: the grasslands, aspen parkland, and boreal forest. It would be more apt to call them the 'boreal forest' provinces, as this is the largest of the three zones, but the intensive settlement of the last 100 years has centred upon the southern, prairie regions.

The aspen parkland, or transition zone between the grasslands and boreal forest, forms a broad belt across today's Prairie provinces, consisting of grasslands alternating with groves of trees, usually aspen, with bur oak and maple in the eastern parkland. The parkland is prairie (slightly rolling or undulating in many places), rather than plain (broad expanse of level land). After the mid-nineteenth century, its good soil won it the label 'fertile belt,' bestowed upon it by agricultural promoters. The grasslands cover a huge swath of the North American continent, from Texas to the southern portions of the Canadian Prairie provinces, and from the Rocky Mountains in the west to the deciduous forests in the east. The land area of Western Canada slopes from west to east at about 5 feet per mile (24 metres per kilometre), which is relatively steep, and this causes rapid flow of the major water systems. The name 'Saskatchewan' is derived from the Cree *Kis is ski tche wan*, which means 'fast flowing.'

Geographers see isolation as the most fundamental geographical feature or characteristic of the grasslands and parklands. To the north is the boreal forest, to the west the Rockies, and to the east a thousand miles (1,600 kilometres) of Precambrian Shield. Only to the south, where it opens onto the vast Great Plains of the United States, does this isolation break down. The description of this land as isolated is in large measure a construct of the culture of twentieth-century geographers – one which sees the 'heartland' of Canada in the densely populated areas of the St Lawrence/Great Lakes lowlands, for example. There are, after all, two significant water routes into the heart of West-

ern Canada – one from Hudson Bay, and the other beginning with the St Lawrence/Great Lakes network. These do
not appeal much to the traveller today, except the adventuresome few, but they did allow relatively easy access to
foreigners interested in profiting from furs. European
activity in fact began earlier in Western Canada than in
much of the American West, because of the access allowed
by these water routes. Yet isolation is nonetheless a valuable
concept to keep in mind when we compare the history of
cultures in contact in Western Canada with that of other
parts of the Americas. The same environment that invited
fur traders discouraged agricultural colonists. In many ways
it can be argued that the region remained relatively free
from sustained contact with newcomers until about 1870.
Just as in the United States, Ontario's frontier of non-
Aboriginal settlement could have continued to surge in a
westerly direction in the 1850s if not for the intractable
problem of the Canadian Shield. Not until the completion
of the railway in 1885 was an easy and efficient mode of
transportation available to accommodate newcomers in
large numbers.

Vast stretches of the grasslands are completely treeless,
although they are are interspersed with highlands, or
outliers, such as the Cypress Hills, Moose Mountain, and
Touchwood Hills. Here there was timber, water, and abundant, varied game. The North American grasslands have
been almost completely transformed through cultivation
and intensive settlement. The term 'grasslands' was really
no longer appropriate after the late nineteenth century,
when intensive cultivation began. The grasslands are
thought to be perhaps the most extensively altered vegetation formation, or biome, on the planet. Only a few fragments of the true prairie remain, and because little is
known of the grasslands' original ecology or function,
much is left to speculation and guesswork. The grasslands/
parklands were home to the buffalo for 10,000 years, and it
has been suggested by biologists that the buffalo were

important agents in sustaining these zones. It is thought that there were four great regional buffalo herds, and that each had its own broad and looping pattern of seasonal movement, following a cycle of concentration and dispersal that was sufficiently regular to be described as migratory. In the full summer months, the buffalo were found on the open grasslands. Because of the vastness of the Western space, they returned to the same spot perhaps only once in every three to ten years, and while they cropped areas bare they also laid down quantities of fertilizer, along with seeds returned to the site. They not only enriched the soil with their visits, but stirred up the surface soil. Their bones also fertilized the grasslands. In the autumn, the buffalo scattered in small herds to the parkland belt, where, in the shelter of the more wooded areas, such as the river valleys, the snow remained soft enough for them to paw through to the grass beneath. The idea that the buffalo concentrated on the open plains in the summer months, and sought the shelter of the parklands and outliers in the fall and winter, has recently been effectively challenged by two scholars. Mary E. Malainey and Barbara L. Sheriff argue that the archaeological and historic record indicates that stable herds of buffalo wintered on the grasslands, and that people, too, had winter camps on the open plains. They suggest that we need to adjust our Eurocentric perception of the grasslands as a desolate, uninhabitable environment in winter. The sheer numbers of buffalo are difficult for us to contemplate today. In July 1869, when it had already been clear for many years to Aboriginal people that the numbers of buffalo were dwindling, the herds seemed immense to a young Hudson's Bay Company employee, Isaac Cowie. His party fell in with 'buffalo innumerable. They blackened the whole country, the compact moving masses covering it so that not a glimpse of green grass could be seen.' Although buffalo dominated the animal life of the grasslands/parkland, there was other game, including wildfowl, deer, elk, antelope, fox, coyote, prairie dogs, and other ground squirrels. There was also a rich array of plant life.

The third zone – the boreal forest, or taiga – extends as a continuous band across North America, from Alaska and the Rocky Mountains to the Atlantic Ocean. It is the most extensive biome on the continent. Compared with the grasslands, the boreal forest was only minimally altered as a result of European contact, at least during the time period under consideration here, although there were game depletions as a result of commercial hunting. The boreal forest is dominated by stands of coniferous trees, mainly pine, spruce, fir, and tamarack. This zone is peppered by lakes and criss-crossed by streams and rivers. A complex mosaic of fens, bogs, swamps, pools, and other wetlands is known as 'muskeg,' a Cree word. The forest floor in many parts of the zone is a soupy, dark-brown layer of decomposing vegetation, often covered by thick moss. The game of this zone included moose, caribou, black bear, elk, and hare, and the zone was rich in fur-bearing animals: beaver, otter, muskrat, mink, and marten.

First Peoples at the Time of European Contact

In 1982 two scuba divers saw something sticking out of the mud at the bottom of Anglin Lake, Saskatchewan, and emerged with a significant treasure: a beautifully crafted ceramic vessel, an enduring testimony to the expertise and artistry of the woman who created it. She was probably of ancestral Cree origin, and lived between A.D. 1450 and 1500. Aboriginal people of what is now Western Canada made ceramic vessels for about 1,500 years before the arrival of Euopeans. Until recently scholars have been content to call this entire era of thousands of years the 'prehistoric,' as though history began only with the arrival of Europeans, and their written documents. Many scholars now prefer the term 'pre-contact.' It is impossible to describe a single 'traditional pre-contact' life in Western

Canada. 'Traditional' implies a static state, yet, as in all societies, Aboriginal peoples were continually absorbing new influences, shedding old ones, and transforming ways of doing things. In this book, I briefly describe patterns of life in the two dominant environments of the Plains and forest on the eve of European contact. This task is not as easy as it might appear. How much has been changed by the devastating impact of diseases brought by Europeans? Aboriginal societies may have had much larger populations. There may already have been a long process of population decline, as well as cultural and social change. It is difficult to know with certainty which people lived where before, and even during, the era of European fur-trade contact.

There are also grave problems with the concept of 'European contact.' Columbus's celebrated landfall in October 1492 is still seen as the critical moment by many scholars, even though we know with certainty that the Vikings settled in Newfoundland 500 years earlier. The year 1492 had little immediate meaning for people beyond the islands that Columbus landed upon, although the deadly pathogens released soon after may well have unleashed new diseases well into the heart of the continent. Just when can we say European contact began in Western Canada? Actual but sporadic face-to-face contact for some could have begun in the first years of the seventeenth century, when Europeans began to sail into Hudson's Bay. For a century or more before that, however, even the people of the 'isolated' Western interior felt the effects of European contact that had been taking place to the east since the late fifteenth century. The term 'proto-historic' is used by scholars to refer to the period of time when the effects of contact were felt, through the spread of disease, for example, or trade goods exchanged along ancient routes, yet face-to-face contact had not taken place. Many Aboriginal residents of Western Canada may nonetheless have never seen any newcomers until the later decades of the nineteenth century. There is no one precise date that can be assigned to European contact.

Plains Life

Archaeological research, oral histories, and documentation indicate that Assiniboine, Cree, Blackfoot (which include the Blood, Siksika, and Peigan), Gros Ventres, Kutenai, Shoshoni, Crow, and possibly the Tsuu T'ina (Sarcee), were living on the northernmost stretches of the Great Plains that became Western Canada around A.D. 1500. Not all of these people remained residents of the Canadian portion of the Great Plains after Europeans arrived. The Shoshoni and Crow retreated south by the late eighteenth century, and all of the Kutenai lived on the west side of the Rockies by the early nineteenth century.

The people of the Northern Plains had widely different origins, and they belonged to different language groups. Blackfoot and Cree are Algonquian languages, so that these people share distant origins, according to linguists, while the Assiniboine speak a Siouan language, indicating that they are relatives of the Dakota (Sioux) peoples. The Tsuu T'ina are Athapaskan speakers, and are related both to northerly people such as the Dene, and also to the Navaho and Apache of the United States. All of these Plains people shared to some extent a pattern of culture and economy. They developed a lifestyle that was well suited to the predominantly flat, treeless landscape, and to the climate of extremes and uncertainties. The key to survival in this environment was mobility and flexibility. Plains people exploited the seasonal diversity of their environment by moving their settlements from habitat to habitat, to find the greatest natural food supply. All aspects of life hinged on this mobility; their tipis, for example, were easily taken apart and moved, and their other property was kept to a strict minimum so that they could be unencumbered.

The buffalo was the foundation of the Plains economy, providing people with not only a crucial source of protein and vitamins, but many other necessities, including shelter, clothing, bedding, containers, tools, and fuel. To rely on one staple resource alone, however, was risky in the Plains environment, as there were periodic shortages of buffalo, and Plains people drew on a wide variety of other animals and plants. It was mainly the gathering and preserving work of women, based on their intimate understanding of the environment, that varied the subsistence base and contributed to 'risk reduction.' Later immigrant women to the Plains would also acquire this role, learning quickly that grain crops were not always dependable.

The most popular image of the 'Plains Indian' is that of a male warrior or hunter on horseback, but the phase of equestrian culture on the Great Plains was brief, and especially so for the people of the Northern Plains. Horses, introduced through the Spanish to the south, did not reach the people of what became Canada until the mid-eighteenth century and did not begin to transform Northern Plains culture until the early years of the 1800s. For millennia the people travelled on foot. A variety of sophisticated methods were used in hunting buffalo, including the buffalo jump (driving a herd off a cliff) and the buffalo pound (enticing a herd into a corral or surround). Each of these hunting methods took planning, foresight and preparation, knowledge of the buffalo and of the terrain, as well as flexibility, and sensitivity to shifting conditions. Each involved complex strategies, weeks of work, and specialists adept at driving animals in the right direction, and at the right speed, as well as spiritual and ritual specialists. Drive lines might extend for several miles back from the pound or the jump. Both methods involved the use of illusion – in the case of the buffalo jump, the animals had to be prevented from perceiving the drop ahead, and in the case of the pound, they had to be fooled into thinking that they were surrounded by a solid wall. Some researchers have suggested that, because of the use of enclosures and drive lines, Aboriginal people may be said to have practised a form of animal husbandry, or domestication. As well, they used fire to help create rich pasturage to promote the increase and health of the buffalo herds.

Archaeological evidence confirms that the people of the Northern Plains practised some agriculture well before contact with Europeans. On the Great Plains of North America, agriculture was a far more ancient and indigenous tradition than equestrian culture. Intensive cultivation of plants spread north into Minnesota and the Dakotas in the period approximately between A.D. 900 and 1000, and continued well into the nineteenth century. Along the Upper Missouri, the Mandan, Hidatsa, and Arikara maintained a flourishing agricultural economy developed over seven centuries. They grew corn, beans, squash, sunflowers, pumpkins, and tobacco. People of the Northern Plains such as the Plains Cree had extensive trade contacts with the agricultural village people of the Plains. Archaeological excavations near the present-day town of Lockport, north of Winnipeg, on the Red River, have unearthed evidence of agricultural activities, approximately 400 years before the arrival of the Selkirk settlers from Scotland, usually heralded as the West's first farmers. About a dozen hoes made from bison scapula, deep storage pits, charred corn kernels, and ceramic vessels were found at the site, which was clearly carefully selected by these farmers for its light soil, and east-bank location to maximize exposure to the hot afternoon sun. The Blackfoot of the Northern Plains grew tobacco in the years before the product acquired from European traders replaced the home-grown variety. Each spring an elaborate tobacco-planting ceremony was conducted, and there were 230 songs associated with this ceremony. Tsuu T'ina elder Eagle Ribs described in 1904 how tobacco was planted, and how the ceremony was linked to the sacred origin of the beaver bundle, a collection of symbolic objects that was the focus of central rituals.

Aboriginal life on the Plains followed a pattern of concentration and dispersal that to a great extent paralleled that of the buffalo, but people did not 'follow' the buffalo; rather, they specialized in seeking out good habitats. In midsummer, people from many social units, or bands – aggregations formed around a prominent extended family – gathered in large numbers on the open plains. These encampments were possible because of the plentiful food source nearby, and they were vital to the maintenance of a sense of community among the various Plains groups of Blackfoot, Cree, and Assiniboine. The annual meeting of diverse bands functioned in the same way as a trade fair, or town, except that the site could change from year to year. Visiting, trading, sports competitions, and marriages took place, and disputes were settled. Trade and military strategy was discussed by leaders. Elders knowledgeable in the history and cultural values of the people held training programs. This was also when the Sun Dance was held, the central ceremony of Plains people, during which the spirit powers were asked to bless the people. This ceremony played a vital role in sustaining and reinforcing the culture and society of the people.

These large encampments lasted only a few weeks, then people began to move in smaller groups towards their wintering territory, in the parkland, river valleys, foothills, or outliers. As winter progressed, congregations broke up into smaller and smaller groups, although efficient communication systems were kept up between the groups on issues such as the availability and location of buffalo. Camp movements were determined in part by the buffalo, but also by considerations such as the ripeness and location of saskatoon berries, the prairie turnip, and other fruits and tubers. Plains people were much more than buffalo hunters. They used plants for vegetable foods, but also for medicines, for ceremonies, in the production of dyes and perfumes, in the manufacture of weapons and toys, and for construction materials. It has been estimated that about 185 plant species were used by the Blackfoot. Women's gathering work was vital; survival of the group depended upon the efforts of women as well as men. Women also were vital to the communal hunt – they butchered, and then dried the meat. Recent archaeological work has suggested that there has been a tendency to overemphasize the importance of the buffalo hunt, and consequently the male hunter, because it is the material culture of the buffalo hunt, the lithics, or projectile points, that remain preserved, while material culture associated with women's work – their digging sticks, basketry, and leather works – do not last as long in the earth.

The Aboriginal societies under consideration in this book are generally thought to have had egalitarian gender relations before the advent of European influence. When collective hunting methods dominated, women's economic contribution was vital – they had access to resources, and power to distribute the products of their labour, and thus were not subordinate to men. With the advent of the horse, and the European fur/robe trade, the male segment of society may have benefited, with women's influence suffering as a consequence. These are tentative conclusions, however. The documentary evidence on women was overwhelmingly produced by European males, who had little appreciation of their roles and ranges of activities. They tended to be surprised at the amount of physical labour that Aboriginal women performed, and often concluded that they were little better than slaves or beasts of burden. At times, however, European observers commented on the amount of power and influence women appeared to exercise – over their husbands, for example. Yet we have to ask: did these observers fail to understand the lives and roles of women, were their views biased by the ideological boundaries of their own concept of proper roles for women (and men), or did their observations to some extent actually reflect the work and status of Aboriginal women? Were these men observing societies that had already been transformed by the impact of European contact? Promoting the idea that women were exploited in Aboriginal society made

Europeans appear so much more enlightened and benevolent.

Boreal Forest Life

The people that lived in the boreal forest region of what became the three Prairie provinces at roughly the time of European contact likely included Cree, Ojibway (Anishnabe), Chipewyan, Slavey, and Beaver. Within each of these groups there are further subdivisions, dialectically and geographically. The Western Cree of the boreal forest, for example, are made up of the Swampy, Rocky, and Woods Cree. The Cree and Ojibway must share a common ancestry as both speak Algonquian languages, while the others spoke dialects of Athapaskan. As was the case for the Plains environment, the uniformity of the subarctic terrain and resources impelled similar, although not precisely the same, adaptations. It must be kept in mind, however, that there was local variability, and distinctive cultural and religious patterns as well as social traditions. Here, too, moving from one seasonal camp to another was a key to survival where resources were so dispersed, game populations fluctuated, and extreme climatic conditions were unpredictable. Human population levels in the boreal forest were always low, and most people lived in small, extended-family groups.

Large game, especially caribou and moose, provided the foundation for life. Big game was hunted with bows and arrows almost exclusively by males travelling in small parties. Fishing was a seasonal pursuit, using weirs, nets, hooks, or spears. Subarctic hunters widely shared certain spiritual beliefs. They believed that the success of a hunt was to a large degree dependent on the prey's willingness to support the life of the hunter, and his dependants, and they sought rapport with the spirits of the animals. It was believed that there was an owner, or keeper, of all animals and plants, and that only through permission of the owners would an individual animal be killed or plant harvested. Women used traps and snares for smaller game, and they gathered berries, roots, bulbs, and young shoots. As on the Plains, the people of the boreal forest took steps to manage and maintain their environment and their game. Through the selective use of small and carefully located fires, they hastened new growth in the spring, which attracted game and fostered the growth of desired plants such as blueberries and raspberries.

People of the boreal forest were not able to congregate on the same scale as the Plains people in midsummer, or for as long. Yet some bands did meet together during the warmer days and weeks at fishing camps, or other rendezvous sites, before heading in the direction of autumn and winter seasonal camps. The rendezvous was characterized by days or weeks of intense social interaction, much of it focused upon trade, social events, and ceremonies. Central religious ceremonies were held at this time, such as the Midewiwin of the Ojibway, and the shaking-tent ceremony shared by many Algonquian groups. Archaeological work at ancient rendezvous sites on the southern edge of the boreal forest reveal that there was considerable interaction, including exchange of ideas and materials, between the occupants of the Plains and the forest people. The influence of Plains cultures, for example, is seen in the pottery of the forest people, and similarly Plains pottery reflects forest influences, including fabric, and net-impressed vessel exteriors. Archaeological sites in the aspen-parkland belt reflect a general mixing and melding of influences of both the Plains and the forest, and attest to the social and economic flexibilty of pre-contact populations in responding to local ecological and social situations.

2

Worlds Intersect

Conventional accounts of the 'discoverers' and 'explorers' of Western Canada used to pay tribute to the courage, fortitude, tenacity, and adventuresome spirit of the first European men to venture into the dangerous and unknown far-off reaches at the very hinterland of the New World. Throughout Western Canada today, rivers and mountains are named for the Europeans credited with 'discovering' them, and statues and schools stand as monuments to their achievements. Especially since 1992, and the criticisms that centred upon the proposed celebration of the Columbus Quincentennial, perspectives on the European discoverers and explorers, as well as on the broader issue of the encounters of cultures, have shifted. The explorers, and those who followed in their wake, are now just as likely to be depicted as engaged in invasion or intrusion, and as having unleashed destructive forces. The European explorers didn't really 'explore' at all. Rather, they were taken on guided tours, often along well-travelled routes. In the history of North American exploration, Aboriginal women as well as men played remarkable roles as guides and interpreters.

'Discovery' was not a one-sided process, and it is possible to examine the contact period from the perspective of Aboriginal people as the explorers and discoverers. Most Aboriginal groups have accounts of how they discovered

Europeans. Often these accounts involve the protagonists travelling to a world where they learn about the eventual coming of white people, and returning with talismans as proof of the journey. These accounts often express a curiosity about the strangers, a tolerance of them, and an interest in their technology. According to a contact narrative of the Assiniboine, four young men were chosen by a medicine man to accompany him on a journey across a large body of water. The leader received specific instructions from the Supreme Being as to the preparations that had to be made. After they had spent many days on the sea, land appeared on the horizon, and when the party arrived ashore they saw other humans, their faces covered with hair, like their heads. It was explained to the travellers that they had come to the land of the white race. During that first night the medicine man was visited by the Being and was told that the white people would not harm them, but would help them. The next day they were shown guns, and over many days were taught how to use them. The Assiniboines eventually returned with some white men in a large boat, with many sails, loaded with guns, ammunition, tools, and clothing. They were eventually recognized as the people who had left on the journey long before. The medicine man said he had brought friends, who would teach the Assiniboine many things, and a council was held that welcomed the travellers and the white men.

Some oral accounts describe specific events and people. The Ojibway are likely describing Pierre Radisson's first winter in their territory, when they told of the discovery of a small log cabin in which they found two white men in the last stages of starvation. They felt compassion for them, carefully conveyed them to their village, and nourished them with great kindness. The white people did not inspire awe, or respect, but rather sympathy, even pity. This account differs radically from Radisson's, in which he described the people of the Great Lakes as poor and miserable, and reported that they viewed him and his companion as 'demi-gods.'

Societies in Contact: Patterns and Diversities

Rather than an Old World discovering a New World, the history of culture contact in North America is the story of how two old worlds, each containing many diverse peoples, met, in many cases collided, and from that time on were intertwined. Scholars searching for more neutral terms than either 'discovery' or 'invasion' have suggested that there was an 'encounter' or an 'exchange.' While the history of the European colonization of the Americas has tragic dimensions, this is not the full story. There was an exchange that involved the intermingling of peoples, knowledge, technology, diseases, plants, and animals, and that produced remarkable changes in both cultures. Of course, the demographic catastrophe that was unleashed in the Americas does not have a parallel among the European population. And there were many different encounters and exchanges that defy easy generalization. For some Aboriginal people, especially those of the eastern seaboard of North America, who occupied land with agricultural potential, this exchange resulted in population loss through disease, warfare, economic and environmental disruption, and dispersal or removal. For the occupants of other parts of North America, including Western Canada, the earliest European visitors and intermittent colonists initially had to adjust and adapt to the Aboriginal world, and to rely upon Aboriginal people for their business as well as for their very survival while they were doing business. Eventually, however, this situation was altered, and it was the Aboriginal people who found they had to adjust and adapt to the Euro-Canadian world.

This latter phase did not begin in earnest in Western Canada until the last decades of the nineteenth century, and between this time and the earlier phase of European accommodation there was a lengthy period of cultural contact that resembles what historian Richard White has characterized as the 'middle ground.' Focusing upon the Great Lakes region, from 1650 to 1815, White described a way of life characterized by accommodations or coexistence between Natives and newcomers; 'with no sharp distinctions between Indian and white worlds.' Each side was interested in what the other had to offer, and they had to find a means, other than force, to gain cooperation between opposing cultures. A style of life evolved that mixed Native American and European practices of economics, diplomacy, and warfare. Intermarriage, the emergence of people of mixed ancestry, the creation of trade languages, the mingling of customs and laws, as well as an interchange of technology and material culture, are all signs of operation on a middle ground. All of these were found in Western Canada, especially in the areas surrounding the trading posts, where there is ample evidence of adaptation to and borrowing from one another. We shall see that, in the history of Western Canada, there were many opportunities to create accommodation out of mutual interest, and times when it appeared that coexistence or a progressive partnership might be possible, but these developments were always impermanent. Yet until the last decades of the nineteenth century, the territory that became Western Canada remained overwhelmingly an Aboriginal world, although it was a world that had been altered and diminished in size as a result of the intersection with Europeans.

It could be argued that, on the face of it, there is much similarity in the history of Aboriginal/non-Aboriginal relations throughout North America. As a result of European contact, all Aboriginal people were weakened by the introduction of new and deadly diseases. The survivors of disease and (and, very often, warfare) eventually lost their land, except for small areas reserved for them, and were subjected to the administration of bureaucrats, and to coercive projects in education that aimed to suppress their cultures. They have experienced poverty, marginalization, and discrimination since. Yet there was actually a great diversity of contact experiences. Aboriginal people with widely varying histories, economies, and cultures had quite different responses to the strangers in their midst, including accommodation, alliance, military and or political resistance, and withdrawal. Europeans also had diverse histories, economies, aspirations, and previous experience with indigenous people. The number of newcomers, the kind of society they hoped to create, and the resources of the environment were important factors in the way relations developed. There was almost always immediate tension and mutual hostility when Europeans arrived in large numbers to establish agricultural economies. In other areas there was a prolonged period of infrequent contact through trade. Europeans arrived in smaller numbers when trade in furs was the object, and they did not immediately threaten the land base, as contact took place in zones of interaction. Differences in the environment and the exploitable resources of a region played a large role in the formation of Native/ newcomer relations. Where there were resources such as gold, silver, and other prizes coveted by Europeans, relations of dominance, and of forced labour resulted, as in many of the Spanish colonies of the Americas.

In Western Canada, Europeans did not initially arrive to colonize in large numbers, and to establish agricultural communities; this process did not begin until after 1870, with the exception of the Red River Settlement, and large-scale agricultural settlement did not gain momentum until the mid-1880s. Until that time, the major resource Europeans sought was fur and later (briefly) buffalo robes. Western Canada's boreal forest and plains did not initially invite extensive settlement. The region's relative isolation, the landscape, and the northern climate ensured that this land would not be viewed as a potential homeland for Europeans until areas such as the American West were colonized. The boreal forest was the first focus of European interest because it was rich in fur-bearing animals, and because the vast network of rivers and lakes allowed the transportation of this resource from the interior to the coast. In order for the Europeans to acquire this resource, Aboriginal people could not be enslaved, captured, or forced into labour, as they were in parts of Meso- and South America; rather, their assistance was essential, as both trapping and transporting required the expert knowledge of those best acquainted with the environment. Nowhere in Canada, with the exception of Newfoundland, did Europeans attempt to themselves engage in these pursuits. The best furs were trapped in the winter, and Europeans simply lacked the skill, knowledge, and fortitude to undertake these tasks. They came to rely upon Aboriginal people for their work as trappers, transporters, middlemen, and translators. They required their geographical knowledge, their mapmaking skills, their medicines, clothing, footwear, and foodstuffs. There was little interest in altering Aboriginal lifeways (except to encourage interest in the products Europeans had to sell), and no sustained attempts were made until the later nineteenth century. Europeans had little or no interest in encouraging intensive colonization that would irrevocably alter the environment on which the trade depended. The way that relations evolved was also determined by the interests, calculations, and activities of the Aboriginal participants. They welcomed some European technologies, once these began to meet their exacting standards, and thus had an interest in initiating and sustaining trade.

Epidemic Disease

The introduction of European disease was one way in which the impact of the European presence was felt with the most devastating consequences, and the entire era under consideration in this book must be understood against this backdrop. Cree historian Joe Dion wrote,

'There can be no question that one of the greatest calamities brought by the white man was smallpox. Those terrible epidemics have been spoken of by our old timers as "the end of the world for the natives."' Scholars have only in recent years begun to recognize the catastrophic impact of disease upon Aboriginal populations. Some argue that, long before actual face-to-face contact with Europeans, diseases had spread across the hemisphere, following well-established trade routes, with devastating consequences, and that this must have resulted in massive death, tumult, and change within Aboriginal societies. Smallpox was the most virulent of the diseases. The exact extent of the devastation is hard to determine, but recent studies have estimated post-contact population losses in the Americas to be as high as 85–90 per cent. One estimate for the territory that became Canada places the Aboriginal population in the late fifteenth century at 2 million. If this estimate is correct, then by the early twentieth century the population was about 7 per cent of its former size, at just over 125,000. North America has been described as a 'widowed' land by the time intensive European settlement began. As Bruce Trigger has stated, 'No other people in history, including the Europeans who were afflicted by the Black Death in the fourteenth century, have suffered from mortality rates that reached the levels experienced by the Native Peoples of the New World in the first two centuries of European contact.'

Tidal waves of infection were unleashed again and again, beginning with what is thought to have been the first pandemic of smallpox, which began in 1518–19. Aboriginal people lacked immunity to 'crowd diseases' such as smallpox, measles, whooping cough, bubonic plague, malaria, and diphtheria, none of which was present in the western hemisphere. The agricultural people of the Great Plains proved to be more susceptible than those who more scattered and mobile. The Mandan, Hidatsa, and Arikara of the Upper Missouri suffered massive depopulation. Winter counts of the Northern Plains buffalo people, as well as documentary and oral sources, confirm that disease also had enormous impact on them. These groups suffered epidemics before significant or sustained contact took place, and they endured about thirty-six major epidemics between 1714 and 1919, including smallpox, measles, whooping cough, chicken pox, cholera, and many others difficult to identify. Serious outbreaks occurred at a rate of at least one every five to ten years.

In the territory that became Western Canada, European fur traders recorded several smallpox epidemics. A particularly severe outbreak that began in 1781 was part of a massive epidemic that raged through western North America between 1779 and 1783. Fur traders in contact with Plains groups estimated that 50–60 per cent of the population perished. The governor of Fort Prince of Wales estimated that 90 per cent of the Chipewyan perished. Records from York Factory indicate that, during a four-year period, one-half to two-thirds of the population of the York District died. Another outbreak of smallpox in Western Canada in the late 1830s killed two-thirds of the Assiniboine, and about 75 per cent of the Blackfoot Confederacy. It was estimated that a smallpox epidemic in 1869–70 proved fatal for about one-half of the Plains people. It is perhaps not surprising that Captain William Butler, who travelled throughout the West in 1870–1 should have called his account of the journey *The Great Lone Land*. According to Joe Dion, this outbreak of the deadly malady *omikiwin*, the disease of scabs, and the famine that followed, marked the end of the era of independence and plenty for his people. Describing the outbreak among the Cree, he wrote:

> The people got so alarmed at the devastating effect of the scourge that they panicked and fled to other camps in the vain hope of finding some solace from friends and relatives, and thus the whole West quickly became a vast grave-yard. Even drinking water was soon contaminated, for clothing bearing evidence of the scab was found in the ponds and

springs. As if to mock the unfortunate people's plight, the dry grass mysteriously ignited in many places burning hundreds of miles of prairie.

Military confrontations and trade networks, in both the pre- and the post-contact era, are believed to have helped spread disease. In his study of the diffusion of disease (smallpox, scarlet fever, measles, influenza) in Western Canada in the early nineteenth century, Arthur Ray concluded that the primary carriers of disease were the boat brigades of the Hudson's Bay Company. There was a greater frequency of disease at key posts in frequent contact with brigades from all directions. In peripheral areas, outbreaks of disease were much less frequent.

Many aspects of Aboriginal life must have been affected by these epidemics. What Europeans first encountered and described in Western Canada may have been only the remnants of once very different and much larger societies. Some of the characteristics ascribed to Aboriginal life – especially the fluid structure of bands, and grouping together of peoples of different ethnic origins – may have been the result of efforts to cope with, and compensate for, catastrophic population losses. According to Assiniboine writer Dan Kennedy, the Nakoda, or Stoneys, a branch of the Assiniboine, were formed after the ravages of the 1837 smallpox outbreak. Gathering together the orphans, the survivors of several Assiniboine camps fled to the west, passing through the enemy territory of the Blackfoot, finding refuge and asylum at the foot of the Rockies. Some scholars have suggested that the effects of disease must have been irrevocably damaging, while others contend that these assumptions tend to underestimate the ability of Aboriginal people to cope with such devastation.

First European Interest and Activity

English seafarers, searching for the elusive Northwest Passage to the Orient, were the first Europeans to make forays into the territory now called Western Canada. Theirs are stories of courage, adventure, and fortitude that should not be dismissed or ignored, even though we can no longer view them as explorers and discoverers of an empty land. In 1610–11, Henry Hudson led the English expedition that located the bay that now bears his name. He and the crew of the *Discovery* were forced unexpectedly to winter in James Bay, where they experienced frostbite, scurvy, and death. They also made some contact with the local Cree, who seemed interested in trading. It appeared that they might have already had some acquaintance with European trade goods. The men mutinied in the spring, and left Hudson, his son John, and a number of scurvy sufferers in a shallop that they cut adrift. Hudson and his companions presumably perished. A year later, in mid-August 1612, white sails of two English ships bore down on the blue line of shore; one of them was Hudson's *Discovery*, now under the command of Captain Thomas Button, and the other was the *Resolution*, commanded by Francis Nelson. They put into the estuary of a river that now bears Button's name, and they, too, had to winter there unexpectedly, as the cold weather suddenly set in before they were ready to sail. They were the first Europeans to winter in what would eventually become Manitoba. Tragedy struck once again. Nelson died that winter, as did many of the shipmates, presumably of scurvy. These voyages had proven to Europeans that Hudson and James bays did not provide access to the 'Western Sea' and to China, and the region was then largely ignored for a time.

It was a quest for furs that next brought Europeans to Western Canada. At the beginning of the seventeenth century, demand for furs in Europe began to increase. A method for producing felt from beaver pelts had been devised. This felt produced the beaver hat, a popular fashion item. It was two St Lawrence–based traders, Pierre-Esprit Radisson, and his brother-in-law, Médard Chouart,

Sieur des Groseilliers, who first dreamed up the idea of shipping furs to Europe through Hudson Bay. They had wintered in the upper Great Lakes in 1659–60, returned with a spectacular cargo of furs, and had learned from the local population about the great potential of the territory north and west of the Great Lakes. They could not interest France in this scheme, and they transferred their loyalty to the English. With the assistance of English merchants, an expedition was launched in 1668, and the *Nonsuch*, under the command of Des Grosseilliers, wintered on James Bay. The next spring more than 300 men, women, and children arrived with their furs, which were carried back to London in the *Nonsuch*. The success of this venture convinced investors back in England to establish the trade on a permanent basis. The English hoped to wrest profits away from the steadily expanding French fur-trade empire, based in Montreal. It was English practice of the late seventeenth century to grant patents to trading companies to develop, exploit, and sometimes settle, on behalf of the English Crown. The result was the 1670 charter of the 'Governor and Company of Adventurers of England trading into Hudson's Bay,' soon known as the Hudson's Bay Company (HBC).

In the standard explanation of the founding of the HBC, complete credit is given to the initiative, foresight, and determination of Radisson and Des Groseilliers. More recently historian Olive P. Dickason has shifted the focus, emphasizing that Aboriginal people were actively involved in trade long before the advent of Europeans. The newcomers adapted themselves to these already-existing trade networks. The Cree and Ojibway of the area between the Great Lakes and Hudson Bay were part of an extensive trade network in which the agricultural Huron of the Lake Simcoe region were critical participants. The Huron became the dominant middlemen in trade with the French in the network, through whom furs from the north, east, and west were funnelled to Quebec. Weakened through smallpox and the factionalism created by Jesuit missionaries, the Huron settlements were destroyed in 1649, as a result of Iroquois attack, and the former trade network was shattered. At this point, Dickason argues, it was Aboriginal nations of the north, not two visiting *coureurs de bois,* who succeeded in shifting trade away from the Great Lakes and towards Hudson Bay. Radisson and the other adventurers simply responded to Aboriginal initiatives.

The HBC charter gave the monopoly trading privileges, as well as the right to colonize, a vast area of land thenceforth (to 1869) known to all but the vast majority of people who lived there as 'Rupert's Land' (in honour of Prince Rupert). It empowered the company to govern the territory, make laws, and even make war upon any prince or people who were not Christian. The territory included all of the lands drained by waters flowing from Hudson Strait, covering northern Quebec and northern Ontario, all of Manitoba, most of Saskatchewan, half of Alberta, and a portion of the Northwest Territories. It was about fifteen times larger than England. The HBC, and therefore Britain, claimed to 'own' this territory through this arrangement, not through wars of conquest. In this way the history of Aboriginal and non-Aboriginal relations is from the outset rather different from that which prevailed in the American West.

The shareholders of the HBC elected a London-based governor and committee that hired men, arranged for the ordering and shipping of trade goods, and handled the fur auctions. This London committee also set the basic policies to be implemented in Rupert's Land, and their decisions were to be based upon the detailed records – annual reports, post journals, and account books kept by employees in the field. A governor was to be appointed in the Hudson Bay area to act on behalf of the London committee. The company decided to establish trading facilities, called 'factories,' at the mouth of each of the main rivers, each to be commanded by a chief factor and his council of officers. Initially the company decided to leave the inland trade, as well as the trapping and initial phases of manufacturing of the pelts, in the hands of the local residents. The employees of the HBC did not have the skill to manoeuvre canoes, or the knowledge of the network of rivers and lakes. They did not know how to hunt and trap; nor were most of them at all accustomed to the extreme climate. For almost a century the HBC remained at bayside posts alone, and did not establish themselves in the interior.

HBC employee Henry Kelsey was likely the first European to venture as far into the interior as the Canadian Plains. He was a young man of twenty-three when, in 1690, he made this trip down the Hayes River, accompanied by Aboriginal guides. But it wasn't the HBC that earned a reputation for opening up of new territory. Most of the European exploration of the lands to the west of Lake Superior was accomplished by French-Canadian traders, searching for new and unexploited sources of fur, and to draw trade away from the English on the bay. It was Pierre Gaultier de Varennes et de La Vérendrye, along with his sons, a nephew, and his *coureurs de bois*, who was searching for the western sea as well as sources of fur, and first set about establishing a chain of forts between Lake Superior and Lake Winnipeg in their travels between 1731 and 1743. The first European trading post in the Western interior was Fort Maurepas, built in 1734 near present-day Selkirk. Aboriginal knowledge and assistance was vital for La Vérendrye. In 1728, Ochagach, likely an Ojibway, drew him a remarkable map of the routes from Lake Superior to Lake Winnipeg. The era of exploration in the Western interior was definitely a joint venture that was dependent upon Aboriginal knowledge of routes, currents, and portages. La Vérendrye's travels greatly augmented European geographical understanding of the continent.

In part as a response to criticisms that the HBC lacked initiative in the areas of discovery and exploration, the company sent Samuel Hearne on an inland journey to the north of Churchill in 1769 to discover the Northwest Passage and promote trade. He was also to investigate reports from local informants about copper mines bordering a frozen Arctic ocean. Hearne was also reliant on Aboriginal guides and assistants. His first trip ended in failure when his companions deserted him, and his second effort was also unsuccessful. His third attempt, begun December 1770, succeeded from the point of view of exploratory and geographic knowledge largely because of the assistance of a distinguished leader called Matonabbee. They journeyed through a huge expanse of territory unmapped by Europeans. They crossed the Barren Lands, travelling westward in the direction of Great Slave Lake, and then northward down the Coppermine River. Hearne learned that his exploratory expedition had been expanded into a military one, with the purpose of making attacks upon Inuit and seizing their copper implements. He witnessed the slaughter of an Inuit camp near the mouth of the Coppermine River.

European Exploration Accounts

In recent years scholars have turned with renewed curiosity to the remarkable rich body of written accounts left by European explorers and other visitors to Rupert's Land. These must be used with caution, however. Many presented a distorted and skewed view of the people and the environment. Powerful social, cultural, and economic forces had an influence on the way they observed and the way they related their accounts of exploration and travel. There were well-entrenched ways of visualizing and representing Aboriginal people, for example. What explorers expected to see and wanted to see had great influence upon their descriptions of the people and landscape. Travel/exploration literature is increasingly viewed as 'a handmaiden of European colonialism – as an intellectual strategy for gaining possession of non-European space and

symbolic domination over its inhabitants.' Not all of these
were first-hand reports, written on the spot. Many were
written some time later, and often with assistance. Hearne's
narrative, for example, *Journey to the Northern Ocean* (1795),
has long been regarded as a great classic of Canadian
exploration literature, but increasingly scholars are unsure
to what extent he wrote the final version. According to Germaine Warkentin, the final version may have been produced by Hearne with the aid of a more literary friend, or
revised by another hand, possibly the Bishop of Salisbury or
an astronomer. Hearne's text had often been used to provide examples of the very degraded position of Aboriginal
women, and Chipewyan women in particular. In a recent
study, however, a comparison of the original field notes
and the final version revealed that, clearly, sensational
additions were made to the text. Carefully excised are
images of Chipewyan women as independent and as having
authority. Negative projections of women were elaborated
upon and made more numerous, and some of these negative images appear only in the published journal. These
types of representations were possibly added on or emphasized to enhance sales of the publication. Hearne apparently admitted that he had to alter his original descriptions
to satisfy the public's desires. There were other exploration
journals of this era, such as those by Alexander Mackenzie,
and Anthony Henday that were rewritten and revised by
men other than the traveller/explorer.

This process of altering texts at various stages of production continued well into the nineteenth century. Artist
Paul Kane's book *Wanderings of an Artist among the Indians of
North America* (1859) has been regarded as a valuable
account since the time it first appeared. Kane has been
cited as an important and objective authority on the Aboriginal people he encountered and described, although
he has also been vilified for his negative descriptions of the
same people. Kane's book, based upon his trip from the
Great Lakes to the Pacific Ocean in the 1840s, was the first

account produced by someone not engaged in the work of the fur trade. Ian MacLaren has carefully studied Kane's orginal notebooks and concluded that Kane did not write *Wanderings*. A whole different persona was created for Kane, of the stiff English gentleman, that did not appear at all in his own spontaneous record. Most notably, a whole layer of amateur ethnological observation was added by the British pubishing house. The Indians were altered to become savages – their violent capabilities were dramatized, likely to guarantee brisk sales in a highly competitive market in travel literature.

3

Fur-Trade Interaction

Overview

Historians used to tell the history of the fur trade in Western Canada almost exclusively from the perspective of the Europeans who were involved. For about a century from the time of the establishment of the Hudson's Bay Company (HBC), the French vied wth the English for control of the fur trade of Rupert's Land. The French, established along the St Lawrence since the early seventeenth century, feared the encirclement of the English, now to their northwest, as well as to the south in the Thirteen Colonies. In response to this threat, the French sent *engagés* and *voyageurs* further west, building posts at strategic junctions such as Detroit (1701). For forty years, from 1670 to 1713, there was a period of military conflict for control of Hudson Bay. The French did not recognize the validity of the HBC charter, and held that it was French subjects who had claimed that territory.

The era of conflict over the bay is characterized by some exciting tales of derring-do, as well as of cowardly behaviour. An example is the campaign that has been termed North America's earliest and most successful commando assault. In 1686 the French mounted an attack on the James Bay posts. A small army of just over 100, with a number of Aboriginal guides, was assembled in Montreal under the command of Chevalier de Troyes, a commander from Paris who had only been in New France a few months. They departed in March on a journey of more than 1,288 kilometres through the bush, dragging more than thirty canoes on sleds, on a challenging route where there were no portages cut between the lakes and rivers. In surprise attacks, they seized Moose Factory, Rupert House, the supply ship *Craven*, and Albany. Two years later, the English retaliated in this see-saw conflict that was ended in 1713 with the Treaty of Utrecht, which granted control of Hudson Strait and the shores of Hudson Bay to the Hudson's Bay Company.

The French took steps to nullify the effects of the treaty by building a chain of posts into the interior, in order to intercept the trade in furs before they could reach the bay and the English company. Largely through the explorations and activities of La Vérendrye, French posts reached across southern Manitoba, and into central Saskatchewan by the early 1740s. Fort Maurepas was replaced by a post near present-day Fort Alexander and Pine Falls, and this base was supplemented by a chain of posts, strategically placed to draw trade away from York Factory. Their most westerly establishment was Fort à la Corne, at the forks of the Saskatchewan. La Vérendrye set about establishing an alliance with the Cree and Assiniboine, and became enmeshed in the Aboriginal diplomatic and military world, as alignment with these groups meant emnity with the Dakota. The Cree and Assiniboine, joined by some bands of the Cree, raided into Dakota country. Participation in one of these expeditions led directly to the death of La Vérendrye's son, Jean-Baptiste, as well as a Jesuit priest at Lake of the Woods in 1736.

Soon after the defeat of France in America in 1760, Montreal-based English and Scottish, and New England–based, traders reoccupied the old French trading empire, eventually reincarnated as the North West Company (NWC). They drew upon the labour and expertise of

French Canadians and the Métis. They quickly began to push beyond the limits of the old French fur trade. In 1778 Peter Pond established a post on Lake Athabaska, and the vast Athabaska–Mackenzie region was now open for business to traders from Montreal. The route inherited from the French was their main disadvantage, compared with the HBC, which had the ability to land goods directly at the point of exchange. The St Lawrence route involved the transportation of goods from Montreal, up the Ottawa River, west to Lake Nipissing, across Lake Huron, over to Michilimackinac, and then to scores of points in all directions. The North West Company adopted not only the route, but also the methods, technology, and even vocabulary of the French. This organization was much more flexible, dynamic, and responsive than the staid HBC, whose policy was set by men at Fenchurch Street in London, most of whom had never seen a trading post or a portage. The annual meeting of the partners and agents of the NWC took place at Fort William, where people with first-hand experience could discuss and plan. They used a system of temporary or flying posts, and relied upon few large permanent establishments. They used different-sized canoes for different conditions and legs of the journey. The NWC devised strategies to overcome the provisioning problems caused by the expansion of the trade further and further west. As importing food was too costly and cargo space was limited, the company drew upon local resources of wild rice and fish. They also came to rely upon the provisions supplied by the buffalo hunters of the Plains – especially pemmican, which became the ideal *voyageur* food. Pemmican was dried and pounded buffalo meat that was mixed with fat and berries and formed into compact 'cakes' that were stored in buffalo-hide bags. The Plains became the great pantry upon which the fur trade relied.

For its first 100 years of existence, the HBC stayed at the posts, or 'factories,' built at the mouths of the major rivers flowing into the bay. In 1774 the HBC felt forced to move inland to effectively challenge their rivals. In that year Samuel Hearne built the first of the inland posts, Cumberland House, a log shack, at Pine Island Lake, and the company began to establish posts along the Saskatchewan and at other strategic points. This scene was further complicated after 1794, when several smaller firms began to compete in the Western interior, joining together in 1798 to form the New North West, or XY, Company. There was an era of intense competition, and a proliferation of posts. Tactics to drive out rivals included in 1801 the North West and XY companies bringing in about 300 Mohawks on three-year contracts to completely clear the Saskatchewan District of beaver. The XY and North West companies amalgamated in 1804, and the era of intense competition ended in 1821, with the merging of the NWC and the HBC, retaining the name of the latter.

Aboriginal People and the Fur Trade

If Aboriginal people were mentioned at all in older accounts of the fur trade, they were invariably described as having played minor and subordinate roles, and becoming quickly and hopelessly dependent upon European technology and supplies. Proving no longer able to provide for themselves, they would have starved without the Europeans' assistance, for which they begged. In his 1958 *History of the Hudson's Bay Company*, E.E. Rich noted 'the marked tendency for the Indians to become dependent on the traders, and the danger threatening the trader and the Indian alike if shipping failed and they became completely dependent on the resources of the country.' It fact it was the English who were in danger of starvation without the fish, caribou, and geese supplied to them by Cree hunters. There is no evidence that Cree hunters were reduced to relying on the English – the HBC did not ship enough food to the bay. Rich's assumptions appear to have been based on a low estimation of hunting and gathering societies widely shared in the non-Aboriginal community. Rich also stressed that Aboriginal people did not respond to the economic forces at work in the fur trade in the way that economists would have expected, as they did not appear to him to show an interest in profits.

This picture changed dramatically through studies published in the 1970s and 1980s by a new generation of historians, as well as geographers, anthropologists, and scholars from other disciplines. They shared the idea that the fur trade was much more than a business enterprise – it was a 'socio-cultural complex' that lasted 200 years, characterized by social interaction between European and Aboriginal peoples, producing an indigenous society. The Europeans had to learn about and adapt to Aboriginal cultures, languages, and lifeways. Long before the arrival of Europeans, Aboriginal people had traded furs and many other goods over geographically immense networks, and Europeans were obliged to adapt to these networks. These scholars were equipped with a knowledge of Aboriginal people not readily available to historians of Rich's era. In *Indians and the Fur Trade* (1974), Arthur Ray trained his attention upon the role of the Cree and Assiniboine in their roles as hunters, trappers, and middlemen from 1660 to 1870. He began with the premise that Aboriginal people were central, not incidental, to the fur trade. The success of this industry required the cooperation of both parties, and in this sense 'it was a partnership for the exploitation of resources ... Although it was not an equal partnership, nor one in which the same group always held the upper hand, at no time before 1870 would it have served the interests of one party to destroy the other since by doing so the aggressors would have been deprived of their supplies of goods, or furs and provisions. It is not surprising therefore that peace prevailed between Indians and Europeans in the western interior of Canada prior to 1870.' Yet this was a mutual dependence that was qualitatively different for each side. Europeans were dependent ultimately only for profits, and always had the option of quitting the business altogether. By 1870 trade interaction had resulted in the destruction of the Aboriginal resource base, and many people were in a desperate situation. Ray emphasized that Aboriginal people, in particular those of the northern woodland environment once rich in furs, increasingly relied upon imported subsistence technologies, and that these eventually displaced most of the traditional ones. He also argued that northern Aboriginal people came to depend upon traders to help them avoid cyclical, as well as chronic, food shortages that resulted from resource depletion. His analysis clearly tips towards the 'rationalist' approach described in the introduction to this book.

At the outset, however, Aboriginal peoples were able to dictate the terms of the trade, forcing Europeans to make adjustments. The exacting demands and high standards caused European traders to improve the quality of their trade goods. Europeans were forced to bargain within Aboriginal terms of reference, and were obliged to develop the concept of the 'made beaver' (MB), as Aboriginal businessmen wished to bargain over amounts, not official standards. (The 'made beaver' was equivalent to the value of a prime beaver skin, and the prices of all trade goods, other furs, and country produce were expressed in terms of MB.) The trading companies also had to learn to give gifts as a central part of the trading process. Ray's overall conclusion, however, was that the economic behaviour of Aboriginal people was *not* sharply different from the profit-driven and market-oriented behaviour of Europeans.

The Cree and Assiniboine were 'ecologically flexible,' with an ability to adapt to different habitat zones, and to incorporate new ideas, methods, and technology, all of which allowed them to make rapid adjustments to the changing economic systems. Before the establishment of the HBC, both groups were drawn eastward as trappers in the French–Ottawa system of trade. After 1670, these allied groups quickly assumed the role of middlemen in the HBC trade. They pushed their trapping and trading area north-west with the assistance of European arms. There is an unresolved debate about whether the Cree, and in particular Plains Cree, were situated in the present-day Prairie provinces well before the European fur trade. According to Ray the Assiniboine had an original homeland along the Rainy River east of Lake of the Woods, while the Cree were a woodland people, living around and east of Lake Nipigon.

The story of the French and English battling for control of the trade is but one part of the picture. Various Aboriginal groups also competed with each other. In the early eighteenth century, a great variety of people visited York Factory, the leading centre of trade for the Western interior, but the various Cree and Assiniboine bands increasingly took over control of the inland trade of York Factory. They created a trading blockade, with a virtual monopoly on trade during most of the eighteenth century. They held the upper hand in this trade, and to a considerable extent dictated the terms of trade. The Cree and Assiniboine traded with interior groups, including the Blackfoot and Mandan, and, as they determined the kind and numbers of goods to be made available to them, they 'largely regulated the rate of material culture change, and to a considerable extent they also influenced its direction.' As the French traders moved further inland, a pattern evolved of the Assiniboine and Cree trading with both, taking a somewhat different array of goods from each.

In the late eighteenth century, the Cree and Assiniboine began to shift southward as a result of changing economic orientation. When the HBC started to establish inland posts, the middleman role of these groups was undermined, as Europeans could make contact directly with the trapping bands. When the fur trade rapidly spread far and wide in Western Canada in the period from 1763 to 1821, the fur companies encountered supply problems for their increasingly lengthy transportation routes. To ensure adequate provisions, trading houses were established in the parkland and Plains belts to receive and store pemmican, dried meat, and grease. The former Aboriginal middlemen began to serve as provisioners for the trading companies, focusing their activities on the Plains resources, and on the buffalo in particular. By the mid-eighteenth century, horses were in use on the Plains and parklands. The Cree and Assiniboine shifted their primary focus from the exchange of furs to the bartering of dried meat. They frequently exerted their economic power and exploited the vulnerability of the Europeans at these posts. The provisioners often burned the prairies around the posts in late autumn to prevent the bison from approaching them during the winter.

By the end of the period of competition in 1821, in many sections of central and southern Manitoba and Saskatchewan the supply of fur-bearing animals had been depleted. Intensive hunting pressure was a main cause, but in the early nineteenth century disease also greatly reduced the number of beaver. Big-game populations of the eastern forest also dwindled. There was an increase in the consumption of alcohol and tobacco during the era of intense competition in the interior, as lavish gift-giving was undertaken to entice trade. Brandy and rum assumed a central role in transactions, although alcohol was never alone sufficient to bring people to trade. These as well as the other trade commodities were now much more accessible at all the new posts.

The Cree and Assiniboine who made the transition to a grassland economy and the buffalo hunt retained an independence from European technologies. They did not, for example, rely upon firearms for hunting buffalo. Guns often required repairs, and the flintlock was not well suited to the cold weather of the Western interior. In contrast, for the people of the forest, participation in the fur trade led to a growing dependence on the trading companies. They required a variety of metal goods, consumed more ammunition, and placed a higher value on cloth and blankets than the groups living in the parklands and grasslands.

While most of the interpretive framework established by Arthur Ray has survived unchallenged, there are two main issues that have been the topic of debate. The first concerns the pre-contact location of the Cree. Ray argues that there was a wave of Cree migration to the west shortly after European contact, while others, most notably Dale Russell, contend that the westerly location of the Cree long predated the European presence. There is much ongoing and spirited debate around the issues outlined at in the introduction to this book between the 'romantics' and the 'rationalists.' Fur-trade studies have experienced a revival of the romantic or cultural-relativist interpretations in recent years. Many scholars stress that European goods were assimilated into traditional Aboriginal ideological systems, and that they had little impact on the practical subsistence strategies of Aboriginal people who did not trade in the same way, or for the same reasons as Europeans. According to this line of argument, historians should not ascribe 'white motivations' to Aboriginal people; rather, Aboriginal beliefs and needs shaped the process. There is an emphasis upon trade goods as items valued for ceremonial and ideological reasons, and upon cultural continuity or change that was directed by Aboriginal values and institutions.

In *The Ojibway of Western Canada, 1780–1870*, Laura Peers takes issue with Ray's interpretation of the dependency that characterized the post-1821 period for people of the woodland, arguing that, even though game and fur-bearing species waned, the westernmost Ojibway 'took advantage of and created new economic opportunities for themselves in these decades just as they had in years past.' She argues that they were never dependent upon the European fur trade, although they were intertwined with it. The Ojibway post-1821 might have claimed that they were destitute, but this was 'more the language of anger and manipulation than a genuine cry of distress.' Mary Black-Rogers has carefully examined the many ways in which the word 'starving' was used in fur-trade-post records and has concluded that the term could mean many things besides lack of food. Often it reflected a misunderstanding, or an assumption of the European record-keeper. Aboriginal people often declared themselves to be starving when they encountered traders better off than themselves, according to Black-Rogers, in order to arouse their sympathy and to encourage them to be more generous. Peers argues that the term 'starving' could have been used by the Ojibway when there was no large game, even though other sources of food were available. She found that the Ojibway 'had a well-integrated seasonal round and were capable of anticipating and compensating for all but the worst ecological fluctuations.' The Ojibway had successful strategies for continued autonomy throughout the nineteenth century, until the era of reserves. 'True dependence,' Peers wrote, 'came with the reserve era, when the loss of land and resources, personal freedom, political autonomy, and cultural self-determination compounded the changes that participation in the fur trade wrought in Native societies.'

Women and the Fur Trade

In the 1980s, film-maker Christine Welsh discovered that her great-great-great-grandfather George Taylor was one of many eighteenth-century HBC employees to carve his name and the date onto an expanse of smooth white rock at Sloop's Cove, the HBC's winter harbour near Fort Prince of Wales. Taylor was the company's sloopmaster, and he retired back to England in 1815, but, like many of the fur traders, he left behind an Aboriginal wife, Jane, and two children, Thomas and Margaret. Thomas became the personal servant of George Simpson, the HBC's governor in Rupert's Land, and at the age of twenty-one Margaret became Simpson's 'country wife.' While their union did not 'have benefit of clergy,' it constituted a legitimate marriage according to the socially sanctioned and recognized customs of the country, or marriage *à la façon du pays.* Together they had two sons, for whom Simpson assumed responsibility. He also assisted Margaret's mother, and referred to Thomas as his brother-in-law. While on furlough in England in 1830, however, Simpson married his young English cousin Frances Simpson, and he brought her to Red River. He had a shiny new residence built at Lower Fort Garry, for Frances. Even with such amenities as a piano, Frances found it very difficult to adjust to life in Rupert's Land. Margaret Taylor's reaction can only be imagined, as she left no diaries, letters, or a will. But there must have been pain, suffering, and uncertainty about the future. Simpson arranged that she be hastily married to a French-Canadian *voyageur* and stonemason, Amable Hogue. Thus Margaret, until recently recognized as the wife of the governor, became a resident of a Métis labourers' camp outside the walls of Lower Fort Garry. The Hogues raised a large family on their river lot along the Assiniboine. One of their daughters, Maggie Hogue, was Christine Welsh's great-grandmother.

The story of this one family exemplifies much about the history of Aboriginal and European marriages in fur-trade country, and the recovery of the story owes a great deal to the work of historian Sylvia Van Kirk, author of *Many Tender Ties* (1980). This book concentrated upon the role played by women in the fur trade and in the development of what she and other scholars termed 'fur-trade society,' the basis of which was intermarriage and the family ties that emerged between the two groups. This phase of intermarriage was by no means unique; in colonial settings in many other parts of the world, intermarriage or intimate relations of a more fleeting nature were common. But in North America, the pervasiveness and long duration of intermarriage in Western Canada is exceptional. Many scholars have concluded that the familial ties that resulted were important reasons for the comparatively peaceful relations that prevailed in Western Canada.

Van Kirk saw Aboriginal women as 'active agents' who had strategies and agendas of their own, responding actively and creatively to new conditions, and not as pawns in the hands of men. European fur traders married Aboriginal women, and came to rely upon them for their skill and expertise economically and diplomatically. Yet these marital alliances were beneficial to all involved. The women may have seen economic advantages in an easier, richer lifestyle, with access to technology that they desired. There were interesting job opportunities for women as interpreters, guides, and cultural mediators. Their families used such alliances to draw the European trader into a kinship network that could bring economic security, preferential treatment, and prestige. For the European traders, these marriages provided companionship, but also economic services vital to the functioning of the individual in a new environment, as well as to the trade at large. Women manufactured moccasins and other crucial items, and virtually kept Europeans alive at fur-trade posts through their provisioning. The alliances made with families promoted better trade. Above all, these marriages and the often large families that resulted made life bearable for Europeans. The majority were lasting and loving, according to Van Kirk. Marriage *à la façon du pays* was an honourable and recognized marriage rite. Men of the French fur trade, and later of the North West Company, had Aboriginal wives and families, and the HBC's official ruling against such alliances was soon unenforceable, and not appropriate.

These marriages, however, were not always 'tender ties.' Especially in the era of intense competition, there were instances of Aboriginal women being abused and abandoned. Later generations of European fur traders tended to marry women of mixed Aboriginal/European ancestry. Aboriginal wives increasingly fell out of favour in the fur-trade societies that grew up around stable posts such as

York Factory and Norway House, and at Red River. The trend is best exemplified by Simpson, and his marriage to his English cousin. Protestant and Catholic missionaries who began to arrive in Red River were hostile towards the 'custom of the country,' and the women formerly recognized as legitimate wives were increasingly seen as not respectable.

Van Kirk's work has been challenged from several directions. It has been argued by other scholars, most notably Ron Bourgeault, that women were exploited sexually as well as for their labour, and that their lives were diminished through involvement with Europeans in the fur trade. Recent studies of Aboriginal women and missionary work have cast these women in quite a different light, not as leading agents of cultural interaction, but rather as champions of cultural traditions. Questions have been raised about whether Aboriginal women *did* recognize and seek a superior technology and/or way of life through relationships with Europeans. Again the question emerges – to what degree were Aboriginal people dependent upon European technology? A further dimension to consider is whether women and men had the same responses. Analysing the artefacts found at a late 1760s 'pedlars'' post in present-day Saskatchewan, anthropologist Alice B. Kehoe argued that, in spite of the readily available and supposedly superior European goods, the women associated with this post preferred traditional technologies: '... some of the Native artifacts were as efficient, or ... superior in comparison to European manufactures when used for traditional Native women's tasks.' A variety of European goods were unearthed inside the walls of the post – beads, tinkling cones, buttons, and metal awls – while outside, clustered along the west and north walls, the artifacts found included awls, scrapers, elk's teeth, and stone knives, tools traditionally associated with women. Kehoe speculated that these were left by women who sat in the shade of the walls, catching the breeze off the water as they performed their tasks.

A study of cloth and the fur trade revealed that indigenous material, especially hide, was preferred over any European manufactures as it had strength, warmth, and durability. Concerted efforts to introduce items such as sleeves for women's dresses proved unsuccessful. While some Aboriginal men adopted European clothing, women did not.

While Van Kirk's study provides us with a window into the women drawn into the life of the fur-trade posts, the vast majority of Aboriginal women of this era were not involved in this way. Yet women, just as much as the trappers and traders, were essential to the trade in that it was they who processed the furs, and at a later date the buffalo robes. It was also the work of women that allowed groups such as the Cree to assume the role of provisioners, as women made pemmican. We have little understanding of the labour, time, skills, and organization that would have been required. Jennifer Brown has suggested that historians continue to assume that 'raw' resources were simply collected from the wilderness in this supposely pre-industrial era, overlooking the extensive processing of goods by women, before they were shipped. Brown writes that, 'given the fundamental role of women's skills and labor in supporting the enterprise, there are reasons for setting a feminist cat among the historians' pigeons and describing the fur trade as initiating (for better or for worse) a women's industrial revolution.'

Recent case studies of fur-trade interaction suggest that there is no one 'fur-trade history' but many. Nor did they end in the nineteenth century, as is often assumed. Competitive fur markets re-emerged in the early twentieth century, and many peoples of the boreal forest continued to participate in this industry. There is a decided trend away from stressing the dependency of Aboriginal people upon European technology, and greater focus upon cultural continuity and persistence. This has been accompanied by a realization that, because of the nature of the available documentary sources, historians have centred too much attention on the European fur trade in their efforts to write about the past of the Western interior. Historians have made the fur-trade posts the centre of their attention, and mistakenly made them the centre of the worlds of Aboriginal peoples of the past. A recent archaeological study indicates that, in the southern boreal forest, Europeans located their posts at ancient Aboriginal congregating centres, adapting their activities to the existing and persistent social geography of Aboriginal people. The posts did not act as magnets for the surrounding population, as historians often assumed. As Jennifer Brown has remarked, 'Many, probably most, native people were only tangentially involved in the fur trade. Even those who became middlemen or who worked provisioning posts spent much of their time at other activities.'

4

Cultural Crossroads:
The Red River Settlement

The Forks

Like many locations in Western Canada that eventually became cities, the Forks of the Red and the Assinibone rivers, in the heart of what is now the city of Winnipeg, has a lengthy history as a favourite camping and meeting place that significantly pre-dates the arrival of European fur traders. Long before Winnipeg became host to a multitude of diverse people from around the world, and the gateway to the rest of the West, it had been a multicultural assembly point of Assiniboine, Cree, Saulteaux, and later Métis, French-Canadian, English, Scottish, Swiss, and many others whose heritages that do not easily fit into any category. People converged here from all directions; from the east, but also from Hudson Bay, from the present-day United States, and from the Rockies and Pacific Coast. The diversity of people at the Forks was reflected in the mixture of languages spoken at Red River – Cree, Ojibway, French, and English – and in the contact languages that emerged as a result of the meeting of peoples. A mixture of Cree and Assiniboine is called Nehipwat (from the Cree words *nehiyaw*, Cree, and *pwat*, Siouan). Michif is a mixed language, still spoken by some Métis, that combines Cree verbs with French nouns, and the speakers generally know neither French nor Cree. Bungee, or the Red River dialect, was used by descendants of English, Scottish, and Orkney fur traders and their Cree or Ojibway wives. By the mid to late nineteenth century, it flourished at Red River. There was a distinctive sound, and a standard vocabulary that was understood by all. Cree words were interspersed with old English, and some French. *Keeyam* meant 'never mind,' or 'Let it go.' *Moonias* was a 'greenhorn' or 'newcomer,' while *neechimos* was 'sweetheart.' *Chimmuck* was the sound a stone made when falling into the water at a certain angle. *Apeechequanee* meant 'head over heels,' as in 'The canoe went *apeechequanee* and they went *chimmuck.*' The names of birds, animals, and berries were commonly expressed in Cree. The 'old kitchen sweats' was a term for the house parties and dances that were the main social events in winter at Red River. Some French words were incorporated, such as *cassette* for 'trunk' or 'box.' Cree slang was mixed with French in the following '*Chistikat*, I forgot my *clé*' ('Oh, for goodness sake, I forgot my key'). The old Scottish word *byre* was always used instead of 'stable' or 'cowshed.' A fire or candle was not put out, it was 'slocked.'

The Forks of the Red and the Assiniboine were occupied at least 6,000 years ago. It was a place where people came together to talk, trade, and celebrate. The location allowed access to the Plains and the buffalo herds, as well as to the resources of the parkland and forest. The rivers provided fish in winter and summer, and riverbank vegetation served as a winter refuge to both people and game animals. The site played a key role in Aboriginal trade routes, with the inhabitants of the region gaining access to exotic shell, copper, and stone items from as far away as the Great Lakes, the Gulf of Mexico, and the West Coast. It was also a staging point for military expeditions against the Dakota (Sioux) to the south, and the Dakota made frequent forays into the Red River valley to attack the Assiniboine and Cree. The Forks also became a major burial site for the Assiniboine and Cree of the region who died during several smallpox epidemics.

Contact between Aboriginal people and Europeans at the Forks began with the French fur traders of the 1730s. In 1737, La Vérendrye reached the Forks, where he noted that Cree and Assiniboine were situated. Here he established Fort Rouge as part of the strategy of building posts along major transportation and portaging routes in order to undermine HBC links with the interior. For the NWC that inherited the French route, posts at the Forks increasingly became provisioning stations, vital for procuring the pemmican needed to feed the brigades travelling as far as the Athabaska District. The Forks became the site of a cluster of different posts, including the HBC's Upper Fort Garry, and the NWC's Fort Gibraltar. It remained an important meeting and assembly place. In the nineteenth century the Forks was the core of the Red River Settlement, but this term was used to encompass the area to the north, south, and west along the rivers, much of which was formed into river lots. Catholic and Protestant parishes up and down the Red, and west on the Assiniboine, were formed in the nineteenth century, and are still part of the urban landscape of Winnipeg.

The Peoples of Red River

The Saulteaux

Among the earliest of the permanent residents of the Red River Settlement were the Plains Ojibway, or Saulteaux, under their great chief Peguis. Between 1790 and 1795 they settled along what is now called Netley Creek (then Rivière-aux-Morts), just south of Lake Winnipeg (about 30 miles [50 kilometres] north of the Forks). This was Cree territory, but they had been decimated in the smallpox epidemic of the 1780–1, and at the time of the arrival of Peguis and his people there were only two small Cree encampments. The Saulteaux hunted fur-bearing animals, fished, caught wildfowl, gathered wild rice, made sugar, and also cultivated corn and potatoes. At Netley Creek, the soil was loose, sandy, and well drained, and there was a longer-than-average frost-free period due to the close proximity of Lake Winnipeg. It was the Saulteaux who provided vital assistance to the first of the European colonists to arrive. In 1812 Lord Selkirk's Scottish settlers were ill-prepared for their new life, and the Saulteaux supplied fish, game, wild rice, sugar, shelter, and transportation. In the 1830s Peguis and his people settled at Cook's Creek, which soon became St Peter's parish, a few miles to the south of their Netley Creek location. Peguis is buried in this northernmost parish of those on the Red, by the old stone church that was once part of the heart of a flourishing Aboriginal agricultural settlement.

Métis of French and Aboriginal Ancestry

The Métis, the offspring of marriages between Europeans and Aboriginal women, were also among the early settlers of Red River, and by the mid-nineteenth century they were also the most numerous. By that time there were Métis all over today's three Prairie provinces, and into the northern United States, but their heartland and central congregating place remained Red River. The Métis of French and Aboriginal ancestry in particular developed a strong sense of self-identity, combining the dress, language, and customs of both cultures and forming a unique society as they regarded themselves to be distinct from Europeans and other Aboriginal groups. (Less sense of self-identity and distinctiveness and shared sense of community emerged among the offspring of Anglo and Aboriginal marriages – those linked to the HBC.) Distinct Métis communities first began to take shape in the Great Lakes region, rooted in the intermarriage of early French traders and primarily Ojibway women. The defeat of the French in America, the depletion of fur-bearing animals in the Great Lakes region, and pressures of American settlement led many Métis to move further west. But many Métis had no Great Lakes roots. In 1804–5, a number of Métis families were settled on land near the Forks, and to the west at White Horse Plain on the Assiniboine, as well as to the south at Pembina, and by 1814 there were about 200 Métis in the Red River area. Here they pursued a mixed economy based upon agriculture, the buffalo hunt, pemmican provisioning (especially for the NWC), fishing, and freighting. Theirs was a hybrid economy that was well suited to the variability and climatic extremes of the Plains/parkland. Like other Aboriginal people, the Métis placed a high premium on mobility, and drew upon the resources of a wide territory, but this was combined with settlement and the cultivation of several acres per family, on river lots along the Red and Assiniboine. The fisheries played a key part in the local economy, especially on Lake Winnipeg. Until about 1820 the buffalo were close enough to Red River so that individuals and small groups could hunt from there. But gradually throughout the nineteenth century, the buffalo receded further and further west. The Métis of Red River began to organize biannual large-scale buffalo hunting expeditions, one in summer and the other in fall, which might include more than 1,500 people.

Selkirk Settlers

A contingent of Scottish settlers arrived in Red River in 1812. The year before the HBC had decided to grant some 115,000 square miles (300,000 square kilometres) of territory surrounding the Forks to Thomas Douglas, the Earl of Selkirk (for ten shillings). He had proposed a scheme for the colonization of the area, using Scottish crofters. Called 'Assiniboia,' the grant was five times the size of Selkirk's native Scotland. The reasons for the founding of the colony, and for its particular location, remain the subject of much debate. In examining the motivations of Selkirk and his settlers, historian Jack Bumsted has argued that the settlers were not victims, pushed off their land in Scotland, but ambitious people pursuing a better life in North America, and Selkirk hoped that, through emigration, Highland culture could be preserved from the forces of modernization. The colony was, however, certainly strategically located to harm the provisioning system of the NWC. The HBC wanted to end the competition that was ruinously driving up the cost of furs. Yet, Selkirk himself had a previous history of philanthropic settlement schemes. The colony could both help defeat commercial competitors and provide a home for impoverished tenant farmers. It could also serve as an agricultural provisioning base for the ever-expanding inland fur trade.

The grant showed no concern for the claims of existing residents – the Cree, Assiniboine, Saulteaux, and Métis. In 1817, the Selkirk Treaty, to which Peguis and four other chiefs attached their symbols, granted the Europeans (according to their understanding) access to the tract of land adjacent to the Forks, in return for an annual payment of tobacco. At the age of ninety in 1863, Peguis published a statement in the Red River newspaper in which he argued that the 1817 treaty did not constitute a surrender of Saulteaux land, and maintained that the tobacco was not intended as payment for land cession. Peguis claimed that at the treaty council there had been no mention of the HBC, yet 'all of a sudden some years afterwards it turned out they were claiming to be masters here.' There was no recognition or consideration of Métis prior claims, and this was the cause of consternation in that community, who regarded the territory as owned and occupied.

Recruiting settlers for what seemed to many a remote area of the world proved difficult, but induced by a free grant of land, free transportation, and the promise of freedom of religion, 105 prospective colonists and HBC personnel set sail in three ships from Stornoway in the Hebrides in July 1811. They spent a first miserable winter near York Factory, having arrived too late in the season to proceed to Red River, and by the following spring their numbers had dwindled to nineteen. They pushed on via the Hayes and Nelson river systems with one bull, one cow, and a few sacks of seed. The people already resident at the Forks assisted these settlers with supplies, transportation, and shelter. Between 1812 and 1815, about 280 more settlers arrived, including more than 80 from Kildonan Parish in Scotland.

The NWC was decidedly concerned about the HBC settlement scheme, and first reacted by attempting to discourage prospective colonists in Scotland. Direct conflict followed the 1814 'Pemmican Proclamation' which prevented anyone from exporting provisions from Assiniboia. The governor of the colony, Miles Macdonnell, was concerned about the potential for starvation within the colony as farming was failing, but the policy also interfered with the provisioning system of the NWC. Neither Macdonell nor his successor, Robert Semple, took any steps to win the allegiance of the Métis. Urged on by the NWC, but concerned about their rights, privileges, and livelihood, the Métis began to harass the remaining settlers in 1815 and 1816. A group of Métis plundered Brandon House in June 1816, where NWC pemmican that had been seized was impounded. Open conflict broke out that month when a group of about thirty-five Métis led by Cuthbert Grant was confronted near the Forks at a place known as Seven Oaks by Semple and twenty-six volunteers. When Semple reached for his gun at one point during his address, a shot was fired, and shooting became general. The governor and twenty-one others were killed. Overt hostilities ended with the merger of the two companies in 1821. By this time the population of the colony included members of a disbanded regiment of Swiss soldiers, the Des Meurons, who Selkirk hoped would provide protection, and 171 other Swiss settlers. About forty French Canadians also came from Montreal. With the merger of the two companies, many displaced former employees and their families converged on the Forks. More Métis families moved northward from the vicinity of Pembina in 1823, settling in St Boniface as well as the White Horse Plains, from which they continued to provide pemmican and labour to the HBC.

Métis of British and Aboriginal Ancestry

Many people of Red River were of both Aboriginal and European parentage that primarily included British ancestry, most often with a male predecessor originating in the HBC trading system. They were generally Protestant. The union of the two companies initiated the migration of hundreds of English Métis from the posts of the HBC trading system to the Red River Settlement. Many settled in what later became the parish of St Andrews. One example of the English Métis at Red River is the large Ross family. In 1812, Scotsman Alexander Ross married his Okanagan wife, Sarah, or Sally, according to the custom of the country, while he was serving in the Pacific Coast trade. Ross was among the many employees of the HBC who found themselves redundant after 1821. They retired with their five children (later twelve children) to a 100-acre (40-hectare) lot and home they called Colony Gardens, near the Forks. Alexander and Sally Ross were married according to Christian ceremony in the Anglican church in 1828. Ross became a prominent man in the community as a sheriff, magistrate, member of the council of Assiniboia, and he wrote three books documenting his experiences and the history of Red River. Unlike the notorious example of George Simpson, Ross and many other fathers were very devoted to the upbringing and welfare of their part-Aboriginal children.

It is hard to categorize people neatly into 'English and Protestant' and 'French and Catholic' Métis. A name such as 'Angus Mackay,' for example, would not necessarily indicate that here was an English-speaking Protestant with origins in the HBC. One of the several persons by that name who rose to some prominence in the colony was French-speaking Métis, identifying with the heritage of his mother. Surnames were often reworked to reflect this identification: Mackay becoming 'Macaille.'

A great number of the early European colonists had gone by the mid-1820s. Red River never flourished as an agricultural settlement before the late nineteenth century, due to flooding, frost, drought, grasshoppers, and other problems. All the settlers were obliged to turn to other resources of the Plains and rivers – fish, wildfowl, buffalo meat. At times the HBC attempted to introduce various schemes to reduce the population of Red River. In 1841 and 1854 several Red River families were sent to the Columbia River (in a bid also to strengthen British claims to the Oregon). Red River became primarily a Métis community. The population statistics of 1870 showed 11,960 residents, including 5,720 'French Half-Breeds' and 4,080 'English Half-Breeds.' The settlement consisted of parishes, subdivided into narrow river lots of about 4 miles (6 kilometres) in length. The houses were close together, near the water. This pattern attests to the central role of water transport, both in summer by watercraft, and in winter when the river became a road for sleighs and dog trains.

The Métis Nation to 1869

With the merger of the two companies, the eastern route through the Great Lakes to Montreal fell almost entirely into disuse so that there was no longer as direct a connection between Quebec and the West. The French and the French Canadians had left a significant imprint, however, especially their assistance in giving birth to the Métis nation, a striking aspect of Canadian history. In many parts of the world there have been populations of mixed European and indigenous ancestry, but it is fairly rare that the situation leads to 'ethnogenesis,' the rise to recognition and self-consciousness of a new political-cultural group. In the United States there was intermarriage, but not the same vivid evidence of the emergence of a distinct people.

Social historians have written much about the Métis, with particular focus upon two critical events in Western Canadian history – the resistance of 1869–70 at Red River, and that of 1885 at Batoche. The man at the centre of these events, Louis Riel, has been a particular object of scrutiny and debate. Much historic research has also resulted from a rising tide of nationalism among Aboriginal peoples of Canada, and from present-day litigation over land claims. Although the Manitoba Act of 1870 promised the Métis that they could retain land at Red River (1.4 million acres/ 567,000 hectares), there are now virtually no Métis lands in Manitoba. The Métis of Manitoba have taken court action, claiming that they were deliberately dispossessed of this land, that there was a breach of constitutional obligation. Scholars have lined up on either side of this debate, focusing on the history of the Métis both before and after 1870.

Earlier generations of historians customarily depicted the Métis, like other Aboriginal founders of the West, in derogatory terms.They were seen as hopelessly tied to a traditional life that rendered them improvident, unaccustomed to hard work, poor farmers, and as a people unwilling to change, being unhappy about the 'new order.' They were also cast as violent, capable of deadly bursts of passion such as at Seven Oaks, lacking in judgment, easily led astray, and full of imaginary grievances – the antithesis of qualitities considered essential in the new order that emerged after 1870. More recent studies have effectively challenged these stereotypes of the Métis. Their small-scale agriculture, combined with hunting, freighting, and other commercial pursuits, demonstrated a flexible economic strategy, one that was superior to attempts at Red River to rely upon agriculture alone. The Métis of Western Canada were a diverse people, however, and no one description of their lifestyle can attempt to cover this diversity. There were Métis (of both English and French ancestry) who

lived more according to Aboriginal lifestyles and languages. There were some that were taken out of Rupert's
Land altogether to be educated and assimilated into Euro-
Canadian society. The research of Nicole St-Onge has
focused upon the Métis of settlements on Lake Winnipego-
sis who were not buffalo hunters; they produced dried and
frozen fish, as well as salt. They had close ties with the Saulteaux, but were primarily speakers of Cree, and had little
interest in the Catholic Church. There were 'bush' Métis of
the north and west who were not buffalo hunters – for
example, those of Dene–French ancestry in the Athabaska
and Mackenzie river districts. There were Métis who had
Stoney or Assiniboine ancestry, and lived in Rocky Mountain country. Even among the Métis centred at Red River,
there were economic and social gradations, reflecting different occupations as well as a variety of educational levels.
There were more well-to-do freighters and merchants, a
small but influential political elite, and men and women
educated in Euro-Canadian institutions, like Louis and
Sara Riel.

The actions of the Métis at Seven Oaks, and in subsequent events and confrontations, were not those of an
irrational and volatile people who were easily led astray
and did not wish to change and adapt. Rather, they were
expressions of anger and protest at the lack of recognition
of their rights. The Métis version of Seven Oaks (to them,
Frog Plain) is in 'la Chanson de la Grenouillère' by Pierre
Falcon, a witness who composed the song immediately
afterward as an expression of pride and national identity.
The English are presented as a people intruding upon
their land, and pillaging their country. William McGillvray
of the NWC wrote in 1818 that the Métis 'one and all look
upon themselves as members of an independent tribe of
natives, entitled to property in the soil, to a flag of their
own, and to protection from the British government.' The
Métis of Red River also increasingly shared a sense of frus-
tration that was directed against the HBC, especially its

monopoly of the trade under the terms of the charter. They were denied access to clerical-managerial postitions, unlike select English mixed-heritage people. Métis were employed by the HBC mainly as 'tripmen' on the brigades to more distant districts, and earned about half of what Scottish employees were paid. The Métis began to agitate for free trade, which would allow them to expand as entre-preneurs and traders in American fur markets at Pembina. Some Métis openly defied the HBC by smuggling furs across the border and effectively broke the monopoly by 1849. That year the HBC won a conviction against a Métis named Guillaume Sayer, who was charged with illegal trading. An armed demonstration outside the courthouse forced the HBC to back down on enforcing its monopoly. All of these circumstances – political, economic, religious, and linguistic – helped to unite the Métis into an identifi-able community.

In the 1840s and the 1850s, many Métis families began to participate in the 'free trade' in furs, including buffalo robes, and in freighting. Many of these families began to spend more and more time away from Red River, and some former wintering sites became established communities in the late 1860s. Until this time, however, the *hivernants*, as these Métis winterers were called, would return to Red River in the spring. The colony remained an important magnet, centre of activities, and homeland. As the 1870 census cited above makes clear, it was overwhelmingly a Métis settlement at the time of Manitoba's entry into Con-federation. The question of whether the Métis were pushed unwillingly out of Manitoba after 1870, or pulled by more attractive opportunities, is at the subject of heated debate and an important series of court cases.

Missionaries

With the establishment of the Red River colony, missionar-ies, both Roman Catholic and Protestant, began work in

Western Canada, although there is some evidence of missionary activity in the era of French trade. But before the formation of the Red River Settlement, the HBC had not encouraged churches and missionary work in Rupert's Land for fear that missionaries, in their zeal to 'civilize,' might wish to alter the hunting economy upon which the fur trade depended. Religious services had been left up to those in charge of the HBC posts. The first to arrive, in 1818, was Father J.M. Provencher, a member of the Roman Catholic Oblate order, and from 1820 a Catholic church occupied a site near the Forks, in St Boniface on the east side of the river. The first Anglican missionary, John West, of the Church Missionary Society, arrived in 1820. West performed services for the Scottish settlers, and the local HBC employees, eventually constructing a church at Image Plain, north of the Forks, and he also ventured out to points further west such as Fort Qu'Appelle. West was not particularly popular in the colony; he soon alienated the more powerful residents of Protestant Red River, and likely many others besides. He deplored marriage *à la façon du pays*, railed against the fur trade, and was inflexible in adapting the Anglican liturgy to the Presbyterian rite to accommodate the Scottish Presbyterians. In the summer of 1823 he was replaced by the more conciliatory Rev. David Jones, a Welshman.

Although John West was resident at Red River for only a few short years, he shared a great deal with the army of Protestant missionaries of many denominations who were to follow him and who came into contact with Aboriginal and fur-trade societies in the nineteenth century. West was appalled by much of what he saw, in both fur-trade and Aboriginal societies. He saw complete depravity, degradation, and sins abounding. 'Marriage,' West wrote in his published journal, 'I would enforce upon all who are living with and have children by half-caste or Indian women.' The woman taken as a wife by the fur traders he felt was treated barbarously; she was not at all consulted, but was obtained from her lodge through a bribe, then was kept as an inmate at the post, and was a degraded slave to the arbitrary inclinations of her master. The children grew up wild and uncultivated.

West described Indian men as strong, athletic, generally inoffensive, and hospitable until under the influence of spiritous liquors, when they became revengeful and barbarous. He was disturbed that they had no settled place of abode, and no 'acquired wants and appetites which rouse men to activity in civilized life, and stimulate them to persevering industry, while they keep the mind in perpetual exercise and ingenious invention.' They made no 'calculation for futurity.' This profligacy led to times of great starvation. West lamented that what 'we value' is so different from what the Indian valued. Among the Indians, to be a man was 'to be expert in surprising, torturing and scalping an enemy; to be capable of enduring severe privations; to make a good hunter and traverse the woods with geographical accuracy ... these are the exploits which, in their estimation, form the hero, and to which the expansion of their mind is confined.' West added to his book, for good measure, descriptions of the torture of captives of war among the Sioux, a sight he likely never saw. The solution to all of this, according to West, was Protestant Christianity, and settlement in agricultural communities.

Missionary work has provoked plenty of debate. Most of the earliest histories tended to celebrate the heroic missionary endeavours of the selfless men who brought the blessings of civilization and Christianity to 'savage barbarians.' There has been an opposite tendency among some to indict and condemn missionaries for undermining and destroying, rather than saving, Aboriginal communities. These opposing interpretations have been challenged by more nuanced approaches. Among those who make a positive case for missionary work is John Webster Grant, who has argued that Christianity offered an alternative to Aboriginal people when their belief systems broke down.

Missionaries were genuinely concerned for the welfare of the people they worked among; they took action to preserve and defend Aboriginal communities, and even challenged the dominant idea of the late nineteenth century that Aboriginal people were doomed to extinction. Many were important advocates, spokesmen, and mediators at a time when government officials refused to pay attention to Aboriginal spokespeople. Missionaries did invaluable and laborious work as linguists, producing dictionaries and grammars that have preserved, rather than destroyed, indigenous languages.

Other scholars have emphasized that Aboriginal peoples may have adopted what they liked about Christianity, in keeping with their customs of exploring, considering, and incorporating what neighbours and visitors had to offer. If they wished to convert, they had to deliberately choose to do so, and no one could force this decision upon them. Aboriginal people then were not passive victims – missionaries simply could not impose their values. Some Aboriginal individuals and groups genuinely converted, according to some scholars, because Christianity was a vital liberating force. In times of upheaval and rapid change, Christianity offered answers to questions about evil in the form of disease, for example. In most of these approaches, missionaries appear as benign parts of the intercultural exchange.

Complicating any one-dimensional view of missionaries is the fact that, by the mid-nineteenth century, a number of them were Aboriginal, trained as catechists, or teachers. Askenootow, or Charles Pratt, for example, was a Nehiyopowat (Cree–Assiniboine) who worked for thirty-three years as a Church Missionary Society catechist in present-day Saskatchewan. He is remembered in family and Cree oral history as a man who helped to instill a strong sense of cultural pride in his people. He used his position to help his people adjust to dramatically changing conditons. Sara Riel is another example. The Sisters of Charity of Montreal, or the Grey Nuns, who arrived at Red River in 1844, accepted some Métis women in their order, and Riel became in 1868 the first Métis Grey Nun, and in 1871 the first Métis missionary in the Northwest. Posted to Île-à-la-Crosse, where she remained until her death from tuberculosis in 1883, she taught English to the largely Métis student population. Riel became an important mediator because of her ability to communicate with the Métis, the Roman Catholic hierarchy, the HBC governing class, and French-Canadian politicians.

Missionaries also have their stern critics. Some scholars of missionary work have concluded that Aboriginal women resisted Christianity more than men, because conforming to the ideal of womanhood, and the patriarchal society promoted by the missionaries, meant a loss of their power and status. Others, including Harold Cardinal, have argued that the missionaries, although initially trusted, contributed to the disruption of Aboriginal life. They helped to pave the way for the North-West Mounted Police, and for the settlers, and served as an arm of empire, forming a missionary 'fifth column.' They worked to extend the influence of the Canadian government by lobbying for the treaties, for example. Criticisms such as these mount for the post-treaty era, and are often aimed particularly at the work of missionaries in residential and industrial schools. For Western Canada a compelling case could be made for the argument that the missionaries had little impact upon Aboriginal people until the era of settlement on reserves and residential schools. Both the Protestants and Roman Catholics were slow to extend their missionary activities beyond Red River. With only a few exceptions Aboriginal people were confident in their religious beliefs and indifferent to the Christian message.

Missionaries were also important for their impact on the reading public beyond Western Canada. They were central purveyors of 'knowledge' about Aboriginal people through their books, such as John West's. Stirring accounts of missionary life in the far reaches of the Northwest appealed to a wide audience. In these books the lifeways and beliefs of Aboriginal people were belittled, and even deplored. The overall impression created was that the indigenous occupiers of the West were members of a feeble and backward 'race,' living in a world of ignorance, superstition, and cruelty. They certainly had no business being the custodians of these vast lands that were rich in resources and could be the home of hardy, industrious people, who would build farms, railways, cities, and factories. Missionary publications provided information that justified and sanctioned the appropriation of Aboriginal land, and authorized the establishment of a society based on social inequality.

Social Relations and Tensions at Red River

At the top of the hierarchy of Red River society were the retired chief factors, and chief traders with their families; they had considerable wealth and influence, as it was from among them that members of the Council of Assiniboia were selected. The clergy of the Anglican Church also belonged to the elite at Red River. Below this were the wealthier merchants and freighters, who, although as well off, did not enjoy the same degree of influence and power, as their activities often put them at odds with the HBC. At the base of the hierarchy were the hunters, trappers, tripmen, and small-scale agriculturalists. By the 1840s there was also a developing racial tension that infuenced status and upward mobility. 'Race' is a term used cautiously and sparingly today, as it is widely recognized to have no reference to anything that is real, but in the mid-nineteenth century there was a tendency to define people's abilities and characteristics according to what was perceived to be their 'race.' Ideas about 'race' were little more than organized rationalizations for prejudice, but nineteenth-century theorists of race drew 'scientific evidence' from skull measurements, weight of brains, and size of noses. Blood was thought to be a carrier of racial qualities. Those who regarded themselves at the pinnacle of the races of the world, those who proudly called themselves Anglo-Saxon, and especially the well-to-do, tended to be the ones who cherished and promoted these notions most vigorously. 'White' was a racial category as well, even though most whites viewed themselves at the time as racially neutral, or the norm. 'White' meant the opposite of what it meant to be 'dark.' If non-whites were lazy, immoral, and cruel, whites were industrious, pure, and courageous. The British were at the top of the hierarchy of races, they believed, with other peoples occupying various degrees of inferiority beneath them. This justified British claims to power throughout their empire. Ideas about classes were also imported into colonial settings, and a mixture of attitudes about class and race were imposed on the colonial subjects. Racial stereotyping reached its peak at the end of the nineteenth century, and discrimination, in some places segregation, was common in varying degrees throughout the world of the British Empire. It is important to note, however, that not all whites accepted these ideas.

A number of historians have attempted to show how missionaries (especially Protestants), and upper-class white women, became the primary causes of social conflict at Red River. In particular, both of these groups criticized the validity of marriages according to the custom of the country, and the legitimacy of the children of these marriages. As a result, the people of Red River found themselves located in a social structure organized by a complex nexus of race, class, and gender. The Anglicans are thought to have been most responsible for introducing new tensions, for railing against the marriage custom of fur-trade society. As church marriages became the custom, wives who could not claim 'benefit of clergy' were looked down upon. The women who had entered into these marriages, and Aboriginal women in general, were depicted as immoral, as unsuitable marriage partners. (The Roman Catholic clergy tended to have a more conciliatory attitude towards these marriages, acknowledging the existence of a marital bond, and regarding children as legitimate.)

By the 1830s some prominent couples of Red River remarried according to Christian rite. Other prominent men, such as George Simpson callously deserted their 'country' wives, and brought over new European wives or found marriage partners among the white women settlers of Red River. Sylvia Van Kirk argued that these newly arrived women contributed to a heightened class and race consciousness at Red River, with their attitudes of racial, moral, and social superiority. They were determined to have no contact with people they felt were beneath them. Many of the tensions that were growing in the colony's elite came to a head in the three-day Foss–Pelly trial of 1850. Sarah McLeod Ballenden, the part-Aboriginal daughter of a NWC fur trader, and married to a chief factor, was vilified and shunned by newly arrived European women, and many of their husbands, who felt that Sarah could not be considered their equal, and should be excluded from respectable society. In particular they persisted in spreading rumours about an alleged affair with a Captain Foss, which were never proven. Yet Sarah Ballenden's reputation was completely ruined; only her husband remained loyal to her. Women were increasingly categorized as either virtuous and pure, or promiscuous and dangerous.

The stratification of Red River society intensified during the nineteenth century. It became important to some families to obliterate any Aboriginal connections. The children of Alexander and Sally Ross, mentioned above, became embarrassed by their mother if she appeared in public, and were reluctant to ride to church with her. The arrival of missionaries and of white women, however, does not entirely explain this stratification. By the mid-nineteenth century, Red River was moving away from sole reliance upon a fur-trade economy. A capitalist economic system and its accompanying cultural framework were beginning to extend to almost every corner of the earth. Fundamental to this change was the introduction of concepts of private property. In Western Canada, formerly public resources, the most valuable and abundant of which was land, were soon to become privately owned. Those who did not appear to suit the requirements of the emerging order, or potentially stood in the way of it, were singled out for criticism by those who did stand to profit. The Métis, the strongest demographically, as well as militarily, became particular targets. They were clearly most prominent among the legitimate occupiers and owners at Red River. Or were they? Certainly University of Toronto Profesor H.Y. Hind did not think so in his tour of 1857. He had been assigned by the government of Canada to assess the agricultural capabilities of the Northwest. Hind found that here was a land of great potential that was being squandered, and allowed to fall into the hands of 'slovenly half-breeds' who had no documents even to show that they actually owned their river lots. A more energetic and 'civilized' group of people was required. Handily enough, these people were beginning to arrive by the late 1850s, and soon became known as the 'Canadian Party.' They were anxious that Red River become part of Canada, and used Red River's only newpaper until 1870, the *Nor'Wester*, to express their views. An 1860 edition of the *Nor'Wester* featured criticisms of the buffalo hunters in general, and the Métis in particular. Buffalo hunting was described as an objectionable livelihood which 'unsettled' those who pursued it, making them unfit for honest, genuine labour. It made the Métis wasteful and extravagant, yet left them in perpetual debt. They neglected the education of their young. In short, the hunting life denoted a rude or primitive state of society, unworthy of people 'pretending to a respectable degree of civilisation.' These views of hunting societies were by no means new, but the vigour with which they were promoted was new. Those who wished to take advantage of the wealth of these resources had compelling reasons to promote a negative view of those who owned and occupied the land. To introduce private property, to dispossess Aboriginal people of their land, to dominate and colonize, it was important to show, not only the shortcomings of the present owners, but the great superiority of the people who wished to accomplish these tasks. In the course of defining the negative aspects of Aboriginal society, cast as the antithesis of 'civilized' society, Euro-Canadians defined what they perceived as their own ideal virtues.

5

Change and Continuity:
The World of the Plains

In December 1891 the distinguished Blood chief Mekeisto, or Red Crow, related his memoirs to Indian agent R.N. Wilson. Red Crow was born about 1830, and died in 1900, and so had lived through a time of unprecedented change. Smallpox, robe traders, whisky traders, the creation of the North-West Mounted Police, the end of the buffalo, missionaries, Treaty Seven, and reserve life were all within his personal experience. Yet he scarcely mentioned these incidents in his autobiography, which he called the 'principal adventures of my life, about which I am not in the habit of talking, for I am not a boaster,' and which ended with the words 'I was never struck by an enemy in my life, with bullet, arrow, axe, spear or knife.' Red Crow's memoirs consist mainly of a recitation of his thirty-three warpaths – military and horse-raiding expeditions against the Cree and the Crow – that displayed courage, clever tactics, leadership skills, brutality, humour, compassion, and generosity.

Red Crow's 'as told to' autobiography reflects the male oral-autobiographical conventions and forms of the Plains in the recitation of highly prized feats of bravery and skill. Red Crow was counting 'coup,' a term adopted from the French for 'blow.' A warrior could best win honour by striking an enemy, and other feats were counted as coups – hitting with a coup stick, capture of a shield, capture of a gun, capture of horses, taking of a scalp. Listeners would know the degree of prestige to be attached to each deed, and which were thought to require the most bravery. The coup tales established and confirmed the worth of the warrior, and his rank among his people. They would know the deep significance of his final words – that he was never once struck by an enemy. They would understand the importance of the visions he had which gave him wisdom and insight. The 'white man' enters the picture almost not at all. Red Crow's autobiography reflects an Aboriginal world in which the new forces remain at the periphery.

A high degree of independence remained possible as long as the buffalo were abundant, that is, until the late 1870s. Horses also enhanced independence. Although introduced through European contact initially, horses were not controlled by Europeans, who did not have control over the buffalo either. The buffalo and the horse became the twin foundations of Northern Plains cultures for the century before the rapid transformations of the 1870s, and reliance upon these meant that there was not a high degree of reliance upon what Europeans had to offer. It is difficult to argue that a 'middle ground' emerged on the Northern Plains of the nineteenth century, although there were some accommodations and characteristics such as intermarriage. There remained fairly mutually exclusive worlds, and when there was interaction it was not consistently characterized by mutual accommodation.

The Plains Cree had experienced great change, and weathered severe crises before the era of intensive settlement, but they maintained their independence. They did not rely upon European technology, and they continued to highly prize items such as eagle feathers, showing the tenacity of Aboriginal value systems. They acted according to their own interests in trade and military matters. As more Cree adopted the Plains lifestyle, horses became increasingly vital, and to the mid-nineteenth century the Cree sought to form new military and trade patterns that would provide a secure supply of horses. They launched small-scale raiding parties, and at times intense warfare on the Blackfoot, which escalated after 1850 as the buffalo diminished and retreated further west and south, out of Cree territory.

The Blackfoot of the Northern Plains

For the Blackfoot of the Northern Plains (the Blood, Siksika, and Peigan), the early to mid-nineteenth century is often presented as a golden age of prosperity and cultural life – when people were rich in terms of horse ownership, had ample supplies of food as masters of a large hunting ground, and had the time and wealth to afford a rich ceremonial life. Yet contact with Europeans considerably affected and altered them. During the eighteenth century, there was dramatic change and adjustment among the Blackfoot. Archaeological evidence as well as origin tradition indicates that these groups were the occupants of their southern Alberta/Montana homeland for thousands of years, although the precise boundaries may have shifted from time to time. They began to acquire horses by the 1730s, likely from the Shoshoni and either by raids or during a period of peaceful relations with this group to the southwest. There is some evidence that the Blackfoot may have withdrawn in a northeasterly direction by the early eighteenth century, returning in the later 1700s to reoccupy lands to the south and west, along the Bow. Plains people had a keen sense of teritory. There were sacred sites that marked the extent of their territory. There were Blackfoot names for rivers, creeks, hills, mountains, mountain passes, and other features of the landscape. Calgary, for example, was a favourite crossing and was known as 'Mokinsis,' or 'The Elbow.' A few of these have survived to the present day in the names of such towns as Okotoks ('boulders') and Ponoka ('elk').

Horses enhanced the mobility that was so vital to Plains life. They improved the efficiency of the buffalo hunt. Indi-

vidualized hunting methods, with hunters claiming ownership of their own kill, grew up alongside, and in some cases
replaced, the former communal hunting methods. This
new effieciency also provided men with the time to undertake frequent horse-raiding expeditions, which became an
important means of acquiring prestige. With horses people
could also carry more food, supplies, belongings, including
special objects such as medicine bundles for ceremonies
and feasts. Medicine bundles, collections of sacred symbolic objects, were the focus of most Plains rituals. Horses
permitted travel over much greater distances, and while
this stimulated trade and communication, facilitating the
exchange of ceremonies, songs, and dances, it also helped
escalate the pace of war, and of small-scale raids on the
Plains. War exploits, as is clear from Red Crow's autobiography, became an increasingly important avenue to prestige and leadership positions. Within Blackfoot society, a
high premium was placed upon male values and ideals of
bravery, wealth, and generosity.

A number of scholars, including Oscar Lewis and Alan
Klein, have argued that advantages horses provided were
not equally distributed among the Blackfoot. The acquisition of horses is thought to have played a key role in the
creation of social stratification. Status differences based
upon wealth in horses emerged. Horses were private, and
not communal, property. Their acquisition was a form of
individual wealth, and gradations of wealth appeared in
what were once egalitarian societies. The rich had the most
and the best horses, and therefore greatest access to the
good things in life, including the largest lodges and finest
clothing. The wealthy could also afford medicine bundles,
sacred objects, which seem to have become more common
after the introduction of the horse. The poorer had few or
inferior horses, and were dependent upon wealthy leaders
for their economic security.

In a recent critical review, Gerald Conaty has argued
that these interpretations share a faulty assumption that

humans display predictable and common acquisitive economic behaviour. These studies do not show an understanding of key aspects of Blackfoot culture, and how
economic pursuits were, and remain, embedded within
Blackfoot culture. According to Conaty, it was vital for the
Blackfoot to maintain a balance between the concerns of
the material world and the concerns of the spiritual world.
'In Blackfoot eyes, success is not necessarily expressed as
possession of material goods or the means of production.
Success comes through access to spiritual power that, if
honored and respected, *may* result in material wealth.'

Horses, along with guns, enhanced the military strength
of the Blackfoot, and the need to acquire horses, through
horse raids, encouraged the maintenance of hostile relations with groups to the south and west – the Shoshoni,
Interior Salish, Crow, and Kutenai. Guns, powder, and
ammunition were obtained through the Cree and Assiniboine, until the late 1780s. At this time fur-trading companies began to establish posts along the northern edge of
Blackfoot territory, and there began an era of sustained
direct contact. Some Blackfoot bands exchanged meat,
horses, and buffalo robes for trade goods. A Siksika band
under the leadership of Old Swan, for example, was central to the operation of the HBC's Chesterfield House,
briefly (1800–2) situated at the confluence of the South
Saskatchewan and Red Deer rivers. Warfare, however,
between the Blackoot and the Cree–Assiniboine, made
posts in these locations dangerous, and the European traders retreated to the margins of Blackfoot territory.

The Great Plains of North America was a place of tumul-
tuous change during the eighteenth and nineteenth centuries, largely as a result of factors associated with European
contact. Many people changed their locations and liveli-
hoods to make the Plains their home. Tribes such as the
Comanche, Ute, Arapaho, Cheyenne, Crow, Kiowa, Osage,
and Dakota (Sioux) took up new lifeways on the Plains. By
the early nineteenth century, a loose alliance of Sioux,

Arapaho, and Cheyenne dominated the Plains to the south of Blackfoot territory. American inroads into the southern reaches of Blackfoot territory in what is today Montana began in the early nineteenth century, and Blackfoot/American relations were characterized by hostility for almost three decades. In 1806 some members of the Lewis and Clark expedition were involved in an altercation with a group of Peigan, one of whom died as a result. It is thought to be this event which created among the Blackfoot hostility towards Americans, and there were incidents of Blackfoot attacks and ambushes upon American traders and trappers. Yet this changed in the 1830s, especially after the giant American Fur Company turned its attention to the Blackfoot lands of the far upper Missouri. This company was interested more in buffalo robes than in furs and gradually attracted the trade of the Blackfoot away from the HBC. They offered superior trade goods, which were brought up the Missouri by steamboat. The HBC was also not all that interested in buffalo robes; transporting this heavy commodity over the long route to the bay proved problematic. Robes included the fleece of the buffalo on the hide, and the best robes were procured during the winter, when their fleece was thick. Robes were heavy, and the Americans had the advantage of the broad and fairly quiet Missouri – a veritable highway to the heart of Blackfoot country, which by the mid-nineteenth century was also the heart of what remained of a once-enormous buffalo range. Fort Benton, at the head of navigation of the Missouri, became the hub of the trade, the 'Chicago of the Plains.' By the 1870s, with the advent of the railway and with the discovery that buffalo hides could be turned into a cheap leather suitable for making machine belts, the pace of buffalo killing was greatly increased. When buffalo were killed for the hides alone (without the fleece), the hunt was no longer restricted to winter, but could go on year-round. Railway transportation also meant that shipments could be made to the East at all times of the year.

Gender and Blackfoot Society

Some studies of Blackfoot involvement with the robe trade
suggest that it transformed the material basis of their society and critically undermined what were once egalitarian
gender relations. Although the work of women was abso-
lutely vital to the robe trade, their stature and power did
not increase as a result. There was an unequal distribution
of income, political power, and prestige on the basis of
gender. Wealth depended upon the ability of a male to
channel the labour of women. Women were valued as commodity producers, and as a result polygamy became a feature of economic organization. Blackfoot chiefs became
notable for their number of wives. A woman could process
eighteen to twenty robes in a winter, and the more wives a
man possessed, the more finished robes he accumultated.
The age of marriage for females declined to the early
teens, and male authority within families was solidified.
Many of these studies point to the conclusion that, as a
result of trade interaction with Europeans, there was
diminished status, power, and scope for economic independence for women.

The documentary sources relied upon for these studies,
are problematic. There remains evidence of considerable
power and recognition of women within their own communities. They may have enjoyed more authority and
priviliege than their nineteenth-century Euro-Canadian
counterparts. According to anthropologist Alice Kehoe,
Blackfoot women were and are believed to have more
innate power than men, because they reproduced both the
human and the material components of the social world.
They played a major role in religious ceremonies – the
annual Sun Dance was held in fulfilment of a holy woman's
vow. Relgious power was passed through the women to the
men. There was a holy organization of women, the sacred
Motoki society (it has survived and remains active today).
Tipis were made, owned, and maintained by women. If a

woman wanted to divorce her husband, she simply piled his belongings outside of her tipi. There was symbolic evidence as well of the equivalence of men's and women's achievements when, in the Blackfoot children's ear-piercing ritual, 'an old woman in imitation of a warrior counting coup, calls out just before piercing an ear, "I have made a tipi, worked a robe, etc. with these hands."' In the same way that men kept war records, women kept count of their accomplishments. Special craftswomen were highly regarded. It may also be ethnocentric to assume that polygamy was oppressive to women; there is evidence that women welcomed other wives as sisters and companions who could assist in the work. In many cases the wives were sisters. Given the numbers of men killed in warfare among Plains people, polygamy may have been a measure that ensured all women were attached to a family. There are also examples of individual women who played important leadership and diplomatic roles, or who were revered for acts of courage. Running Eagle was a Peigan woman who led many successful horse raids and war parties, and another Peigan, Calf Old Woman, sat as a warrior in Blackfoot councils.

Among the Blackfoot there was a unique role for some women called the *ninauposkitzipxpe*, or 'manly hearted women.' This was a small group of mature, married women, who possessed traits that were considered masculine – aggression, independence, ambition, confident sexuality, and property ownership. They acted in contrast to the ideal attributes of Blackfoot women, submission and modesty. Manly hearted women by contrast were not shy; they made speeches at public occasions, talked freely to men, and used profane language. They did not, however, wear men's clothing, but very fine examples of women's clothing, taking an unusual interest in their appearance. Manly hearted women also excelled in feminine occupations, and were considered very hard-working. One explanation for manly hearts is that it was a cultural strategy that preserved the social and economic stratification of the sexes, allowing only certain women access to male power and resources in male-defined ways. The manly heart identity preserved the male-dominant structure of society by allowing a very few women the ability to exhibit non-feminine characteristics, while married, and continuing to be seen as women.

Confronting New Forces and Violent Encounters

Blackfoot territory straddled the international border, and as a result their history is one of contending not only with British, then Canadian business, institutions, and settlers, but also American business, government, military, and gold miners. They were also introduced to railways at an earlier time than those whose homeland was more to the north. They were certainly involved in more violent confrontations. The Blood winter count details some of these, as in 1839, when Chief White Calf was killed by a white man at Fort Benton, and 1844, when a white man at Fort Benton fired a cannon and killed thirteen Blackfoot.

The Blackfoot were greatly affected by both American and later Canadian government policies and initiatives. By the 1840s the Blackfoot were experiencing the pressures of invasion – of not only whites, but other Aboriginal groups forced out of their territory further to the east. These forces can be traced to the policy pursued under the administration of President Andrew Jackson in the 1830s, that of the 'removal' of the eastern and southern tribes across the Mississippi River. There was supposedly to be a permanent 'Indian territory' where non-Aboriginal people could enter only with permission, and under federal supervision, but this policy soon fell victim to American expansion. In the 1840s the Americans acquired Oregon (1846), and California (1848), and the result was that, in the hundreds, then in the thousands, settlers travelled across the Great Plains, causing resentment and tension. In an effort to reduce tension and to gain the right to build roads and posts across the Northern and Central Plains, the American government entered into treaties with the Aboriginal nations. Until the International Boundary was surveyed in 1874, the Blackfoot of the Northern Plains were active participants in some of these treaties. In 1855, Lame Bull's treaty was made with the North Peigan, South Peigan, Blackfoot, and Blood. It was a peace treaty that defined the territory for the Blackfoot nation, and was to allow for the building of railways and roads. In return, the Blackfoot were promised an annual distribution of goods and provisions for ten years, and they were also promised assistance in the establishment of agricultural and mechanical pursuits. Although some individuals were interested in the farming experiment, government support foundered by the early 1860s, and other promises such as annuities were not kept.

The Blackfoot also experienced gold-mining invasion of their territory; there were rumours of fabulous strikes along the Teton, Marias, Milk, Oldman, and Bow rivers, and by 1859 numerous parties were searching for gold. In response to these incursions there were a number of violent incidents. The inhabitants of the newly created Montana territory began to demand federal military protection, and following the end of the Civil War in 1865 the Americans began to garrison Montana. These were exceedingly violent times on the Northern Plains. Fort Benton, like places such as the Red River Settlement, was home to an array of people, not only diverse Americans, but Canadians, Métis, Irish, and others who worked as hunters, freighters, bullwackers, muleskinners, and 'wolfers' who poisoned buffalo carcasses to kill wolves for which there was a market. Alcohol escalated tensions, was often an invitation for violence, and was a central factor in helping to populate the scaffolds and graveyards of the West. Both Aboriginal and non-Aboriginal seem to have liberally indulged (although both groups had their abstainers as well). Whisky was used in the 'Indian trade,' but more often it was pure alcohol diluted with other ingredients to form a fiery, cheap concoction. It contributed to violence within communities and families, and between Aboriginal and whites.

The 'Baker Massacre' of 1870 is among the most notorious of many incidents of violent confrontation between the military and the Blackfoot. In retaliation for the death of two white men near Fort Benton in 1869, two innocent Blackfoot were gunned down on the street in Benton. Over the next six months the Peigan leader Mountain Chief retaliated in turn with raids that claimed about two dozen lives. There were calls for military reprisal, and a Major Eugene Baker was ordered to attack Mountain Chief and his band. In January 1870, Baker (reported to have been drunk), and four companies of Second Cavalry and two infantry troops, attacked the wrong group – an unsuspecting band under the leadership of Peigan chief Heavy Shield, people innocent of any involvement in the events. The toll was 173 Peigan dead, including 53 women and children. Most of the survivors of this took up permanent residence on the Canadian side of the border, later settling on the Peigan reserve near Pincher Creek.

Whoop-Up Country

The Cypress Hills were within what was known from the late 1860s as 'Whoop-Up' country, where American whisky traders set up operations. Posts north of the forty-ninth parallel had names such as Forts Whoop-Up, Slideout, Standoff, Robbers Roost, and Whiskey Gap. While the activities of the whisky traders clearly affected the Cree and Assiniboine, as well as Mountain Stoneys, the centre of their operations was squarely within Blackfoot land. When Montana territory was garrisoned, the military began to police the trade in alcohol to some extent, and the result was that some of the trade was pushed to the north. They not only traded whisky; by 1870, the Americans were also supplying the Blackfoot with rapid-firing weapons of the latest design.

There were about forty whisky posts in what is today southern Alberta. The result, according to American historian Paul F. Sharp in his book *Whoop-Up Country*, was that 'the region north of Fort Benton became one of the most lawless areas on the frontier.' Sharp pointed out that many of the whisky-trading stories that emerged from Whoop-Up country were wild yarns, and pure myths, and that sometimes interests such as the HBC, missionaries, and Canadian government officials had reason to portray the activities of the American traders in the worst possible light. Many of the stories 'combined fact with fiction so adroitly that to winnow the grains of truth from the chaff of exaggeration is virtually impossible.' There are those who protested at the time, and still insist that the American traders were not hard-bitten, lawless 'bad men,' but upstanding family men. Whisky trader D.W. Davis, however (who later went on to become one of Alberta's first members of Parliament), certainly displayed a cavalier attitude in a letter he wrote from Whoop-Up country to his father in 1873. 'Work is not without its danger as it is trading with Indians altho I have never been hurt or scared yet had to kill 2 last winter on act of stealing horses.' While it is difficult to sort through the folklore, and reach agreement on many aspects of the history of Whoop-Up country, it seems clear that the trade was damaging to the Blackfoot. The arrival of the whisky traders also coincided with the deadly small pox outbreak of 1869. About 1,200 members of the Blackfoot nation are believed to have perished in the epidemic, which carried off many of their leaders. Armed with repeating rifles, however, the Blackfoot remained militarily strong, despite all of the destructive forces.

In June 1873, in the Cypress Hills of southwestern Saskatchewan, a camp of Assiniboine was attacked by wolfers from Fort Benton. In search of the people who had stolen their horses, the wolfers arrived at the trading posts of Abe Farwell and Moses Solomon, representing American companies from Fort Benton. Little Soldier's band of forty lodges of Assiniboine was camped near the posts. The wolfers were informed that these people had not stolen their horses, but they spent the evening drinking, as did some of the Assiniboine, and the next day, convinced that one of their horses was missing, they grabbed their rifles and proceeded to the Assiniboine camp. There was indiscriminate fire at the camp with repeating rifles, and many were shot as they fled. There were atrocities committed on the dead, and some of the women were repeatedly assaulted. There is uncertainty about how many died – one estimate is twenty. However, according to Assiniboine elder Dan Kennedy, who knew people who were there, eighty were slain.

The End of the Buffalo

The Assiniboine of that camp of death had experienced a very hard winter. Buffalo were becoming increasingly scarce in Cree and Assiniboine territory by the early 1870s, and by the end of the decade the buffalo had disappeared from Blackfoot land. As early as the 1850s, the Plains Cree reported that there were only a few buffalo ranging between the north and south branches of the Saskatchewan, and they were trying to protect the remnants of the herds from Métis and other hunters. In the Blood winter count, 1880 was listed as 'buffalo are no more,' and in the Peigan winter count, the same year was 'when they built the first houses,' indicating the dramatic transformations that took place in these years. Buffalo had been retreating further and further west since the early decades of the nineteenth century, a development obvious and worrisome to all Plains people. The retreat of the buffalo from the Red River Settlement was clearly noticeable from 1820. There were almost no buffalo at all in what is today Manitoba by about mid-century, and, twenty years later, there were very few in what is today Saskatchewan. The virtual extermination of the buffalo in Canada preceeded the final slaughter in the northwestern United States by a few years, as they were finally extinct there in 1883.

The reasons for the extermination of the buffalo have been and continue to be the subject of much debate. Among the earliest of the non-Aboriginal theories was that it was the work of divine providence in order to hasten the civilization of the Indian. Methodist missionary John McDougall wrote that 'the great herds of buffalo, as abused by man were hurtful to himself, and therefore in the fullness of time the Great Father, in the interests of His children, wiped them from the face of the earth.' American zoologist W.T. Hornaday, writing in the 1880s, argued that the disappearance of the buffalo was due to the 'reckless improvidence' of the Indian and Métis hunters, who engaged in 'appalling slaughter' and had wantonly destroyed their own source of food.

Recent studies have focused on the role of the U.S. army, suggesting that the extermination of the buffalo was the result of a well-calculated policy to subdue Native Americans and drive them onto reserves. By employing and providing assistance to non-Aboriginal buffalo hunters, by routinely sponsoring and outfitting civilian hunting expeditions that slaughtered on a massive scale, and by encouraging troops to kill large numbers of buffalo using artillery and cannon, the U.S. army, according to some scholars, systematically destroyed the buffalo. There is some evidence that the U.S. army set fires along the forty-ninth parallel in the late 1870s, as part of the campaign to prevent the buffalo moving north and thus in order to subdue Sitting Bull and his people, who had taken refuge across the border in 1876. These fires may, however, have been set by commercial hunters trying to manage the herds' movement. Commercial hide hunters, using high-powered long-range rifles, clearly dealt a final blow. There is evidence that one hunter alone killed 6,200 buffalo in the winter of 1880. The demands of an expanding capitalist market system played a role in the destruction of the buffalo.

Aboriginal people deplored the wasteful slaughter of the hunters, who skinned the animals and left the rest untouched to rot. In the summer of 1870, Assiniboine Dan Kennedy vividly remembered coming across acres and acres of dead buffalo in the Cypress Hills, and he recalled the elders voicing their indignation and anger. In later years, Kennedy was told by a former member of the North-West Mounted Police that the buffalo killers were sent out by the U.S. government in order to starve the Indians into submission. Alberta historian (and Canadian Pacific Railway engineer) Frank Roe, in a monumental 1951 study of the North American buffalo, argued that the Aboriginal hunters of the Plains created a dynamic ecological equilibrium between themselves and the vast buffalo herds, that they developed sustainable hunting practices which maintained the herds and permitted future generations to follow the same way of life. Disappearance of the buffalo had to do with the slaughter on a massive scale brought on by the presence of non-Aboriginals.

Historian Dan Flores, however, argues that Native American hunters (of the Southern Plains) began to harvest the buffalo at about twice the rate they would have for subsistence once they became entwined in the European market system, adding critical stress to the buffalo resource. They were not working out an ecological equilibrium, but rather killed buffalo at an unsustainable rate. Flores argues that the religious beliefs of Plains people may have contributed to the conviction that the buffalo were an infinite resource, an idea that limited the understanding of bison ecology. Similar arguments have been advanced for the extermination of the Canadian buffalo. These perspectives represent a resurgence of cultural relativism, but they are difficult to sustain as there is considerable evidence that Plains people were acutely aware of the dwindling supplies of buffalo by mid-century. There is also evidence that the numbers of buffalo were beginning to drop in the earlier decades of the nineteenth century, not only from hunting but from a combination of other factors, including disease, drought, habitat destruction, and competition from newly introduced species, most notably the horse. The new domestic livestock introduced diseases such as tuberculosis and brucellosis to the buffalo.

There are conflicting points of view over the issue of whether Aboriginal hunters *did* contribute to overhunting and the extermination of the species. Some authorities contend that Plains people had a reverence for the land and its resources, and an ecological awareness that resulted from their understanding of, and intimate relationship with, their environment. Nature did not exist as a collection of commodities; rather, plants, animals and other resources were endowed with symbolic and religious significance. Waste or immoderate harvest was both offensive and dangerous, as the spirits or spirit wardens could exact punishment. Some of these scholars share the belief that in our day there is much to be learned from the wisdom of Aboriginal societies in their attitudes to land and resources – they were by far superior custodians as measured against the immigrants who believed that nature could and should be controlled and manipulated.

Others contend that the image of Aboriginal people as environmentalists is the romantic creation of the modern environmental movement, and that there was no environmental ethic or wisdom, or at least not one that survived the introduction of market forces and the technology that allowed hunting on a large scale. If there is middle ground in this debate, it is occupied by historian Richard White, who argues that it is an 'immense condescension' to venerate Aboriginal people for their essential connection to nature, and to assume that they were 'primal ecologists' who moved across the land without altering it. This view demeans Aboriginal people and deprives them of culture. We need to understand how people viewed and used their environment, and how this changed over time. Aboriginal people did seek to order and control the natural world, although not in the same way, or with the same tools, as the Europeans. They used fire to transform and alter the landscape, and there was hoe agriculture. Yet before the advent of Europeans, there was a fundamentally different attitude towards resources and game, and much of this survived in the post-contact era. Hunting was holy, and it had a depth and complexity foreign to Europeans. Aboriginal people killed animals, and sometimes overhunted 'but did so,' in the words of White, 'within the context of a moral universe that both they and the animals inhabited. They conceived of animals as having, not rights – that's the wrong word, but *powers.*'

Years of Starvation

The disappearance of the buffalo resulted in widespread suffering, destitution, and famine during the 1870s and the 1880s. While there had been temporary buffalo shortages in the past that were coped with, this was unlike the devastation brought about by the final end of this resource. The Plains Cree and the Assiniboine felt the earliest effects of the end of the buffalo and by the early 1870s there were reports of appalling conditions of poverty and starvation. The smallpox epidemic of 1869–70 coninicided with the beginning of what Cree historian Joe Dion called the 'great famine.' In his district more than sixty children perished that winter. Further to the west, suffering became severe by the last years of the decade. Oblate missionary Leon Doucet, stationed in Blackfoot country, called the winter of 1878–9 the 'beginning of the great famine.' He recorded that there were bodies of the dead all around him, some in their lodges, others in trees or on scaffolding. The worst of this seemed to be over by the early 1880s, but by this time government officials also took steps to suppress or downplay information about the extent of hunger in the Northwest. From time to time such information emerged, however. In the winter of 1887–8, for example, the public learned through a Roman Catholic priest that more than 100 Cree and Ojibway died of starvation on the Canadian side of Turtle Mountain in Manitoba.

The great independence and freedom that Plains people had enjoyed came to an end with the disappearance of the buffalo. In the 1870s they faced an extremely uncertain future, but there had been an awareness for years that their economy was no longer secure, that alternatives would have to be explored. As early as the 1850s foreign travellers to the Plains reported that the Cree and the Nakoda were concerned about the scarcity of buffalo, and many expressed a willingness to try agriculture, and wanted assistance in the way of instruction and technology. During the treaty negotiations of the 1870s, Plains people sought government aid to make the transition to an agricultural economy. They were not, however, prepared to embrace other ideas that the newcomers had to offer. Confidence in their own lifeways and teachings persisted, despite all of the upheavel and change of the nineteenth century.

6

Canada's Colony and the Colonized

Historians of Western Canada have been reluctant to consider that what took place here was part of a global pattern of intensified conflict over land and resources. Rather, the dominant narrative has stressed the unique nature of the society that has taken root, devising Western Canada's own brand of 'exceptionalism.' Historians tended to assign good marks to what they see as the orderly and peaceful development of the West through sound federal preparatory measures (national policies): the treaties, the North-West Mounted Police, the railway, and Dominion lands policy. All of these strategies were wisely devised and set in place well before the pressures of intensive settlement began. Bad marks are assigned to the United States for what is seen as their more disorderly, violent, militaristic approaches to domestic issues. These assumptions are central to the way Western Canadians have identified themselves, to the virtues that they ascribe to themselves, even though the American comparison is rarely considered in detail. Yet Western Canada was the site of two major military expeditions, one in 1870 and another in 1885. They were both sent to quell 'uprisings' of Aboriginal people. The first arrived too late for actual military confrontation, but the second, the largest mobilization ever to take place on Canadian soil, engaged in battle with Aboriginal people, mainly Métis. Not only do these events challenge assumptions about Canada's peaceful West, they also clearly have parallels to other such challenges to colonial authority in other settings. The Victorian British army was central to the defence of the empire, and the military expeditions to the heart of Western Canada were led by British officers. The 1870 expedition was led by Lord Garnet Wolseley, one of the great commanders of the late nineteenth century who served in Burma, the Crimea, India, China, Egypt, the Sudan, and South Africa. Major General Frederick Middleton, who commanded the North-West Field Force in 1885, had earned medals in the 'India Mutiny,' and in 'small warfare' in New Zealand. It is helpful for Western Canadian historians not only to study the local, but to see how this fits into larger patterns of colonialism and empire.

It is by no means new to say that Western Canada was a colony. There have been generations of scholars, as well as politicians, who have lamented that the Prairie West was an economic and political colony of the federal government. In this scenario it is the immigrants who began to arrive in the late nineteenth century who are the colonized, governed by distant and insensitive politicians and administrators. It is not as common, however, to see Canada's relationship with Aboriginal people within a colonial framework. Alberta-born historian G.F.G. Stanley, who published the influential *Birth of Western Canada* in 1935, was unique in his interpretation of the Métis response to colonization as part of a global pattern of the resistance of indigenous people. Reflecting the widely held view of his generation, however, Stanley saw these as uprisings of uncivilized people, who sought to preserve a primitive way of life, and were inevitably unable to sustain resistance againt superior people.

Recognizing that 'colonialism' is a term that refers to a great variety of asymmetrical relationships, and that colonial rule is highly varied in administration and impact, some broad similiarities may be identified. Fundamental features of colonialism were present in Western Canada in the late nineteenth century, including the extension of the power of the Canadian state, and the maintenance of sharp social, economic, and spatial distinctions between the dominant and subordinate population. Colonial rule involved the domination, or attempted domination, of an expatriate group over indigenous people. The colonies were generally run by the whites, sometimes in association with indigenous 'collaborators,' for their own power and profit. The commercial enterprise of the expatriates was facilitated by colonial administrators, and typically the indigenous people lost a good proportion of their land. When the indigenous people attempted to participate in or compete with these commercial enterprises, their efforts were often thwarted by the combined efforts of entrepreneurs and colonial administrators. Indigenous leadership and authority, along with the independence of the original inhabitants, were thus eroded, and the rebellions that so often resulted were typically met with overwhelming force.

From Frozen Wilderness to Blooming Garden

In 1849 the British colonial secretary summarized his views on Rupert's Land. 'How a country where there is eight months [of] winter, and snow on the ground for the whole period, is to be opened up, is to me a riddle.' In a few short years, however, this image of Western Canada as an inhospitable wilderness, suited only to the fur trade, with little to offer agriculturalists, was remarkably transformed. Before very long, the very same landscape, or at least parts of it, viewed from the perspective of developers and 'expansionists'(those who wanted to extend Canada's influence over Rupert's Land), was transformed into a fertile garden. The 1850s marks a crucial change in the image of the West from a wilderness to a potential home. These images, of course, represent the non-Aboriginal viewpoint. The original occupants had never seen their homeland as a fur-trade hinterland, or inhospitable wilderness; nor was there any dramatic transformation after 1850 to a new view of the rich agricultural and resource potential, although they were becoming keenly aware that their homeland was viewed in this way by outsiders.

Concern about American expansion westward, heightened by the Oregon dispute of 1846, which extended the border of the forty-ninth parallel to the Pacific coast, caused British officials to begin considering the possibilities for colonization in Rupert's Land. Critics of the HBC monopoly argued that the company could not be an effective agent of colonization, as its commercial interests made this impossible. The HBC charter was up for renewal in 1859, and a British parliamentary committee was convened to consider whether the status quo should be continued, or the charter revoked as a step towards a more vigorous promotion of settlement. There were also signs of increasing social and political unrest in Red River, with the successful Guillaume Sayer trial of 1849 in which the Métis displayed their own clout in the settlement. These developments coincided with the activities of the expansionists of Canada West who were convinced that acquisition of these territories was vital to the future prosperity of Canada and the British Empire. But Canadians had to be persuaded that the territory was of any value. This was accomplished through two expeditions sent in 1857, one under the auspices of the Canadian government led by Henry Youle Hind, and the other sent by the British government under the command of Captain John Palliser. Hind and Palliser agreed that there was an area of arid and treeless country to the south that was not suitable for agriculture, but that there was an extensive fertile belt of parkland country that was. This fertile-belt concept gave the expansionists what they needed to bolster their optimistic appraisals.

The expansionists mustered economic arguments that appealed to the pocketbook, but there were also appeals to emotion, to patriotism and pride. Hind reflected some of this zeal when he wrote of the great grandeur and beauty of the West. This was a project of enormous scale that would create a properous region, in turn profiting the older regions of Canada, especially Ontario. There was talk of dominion from sea to sea, and of a railway that could link the far-flung regions to the rest of Canada. Part of the rhetoric of expansion was the opportunity to extend British influence, to shape and mould a society based on British stock, British customs, and Protestantism. It was not to be a French and Roman Catholic society; nor was it to be a Métis society. Hind argued that the Métis were in fact a retarding influence. There was nothing wrong with the soil and the climate of the West, according to Hind. What was wrong was that it was occupied by a flawed people who had not energetically harnessed the resources available to them. The Métis preferred the wild life of the prairies to a settled home anyway, and they had no prior claim, in Hind's opinion.

Expansionists expressed some interest in the future of the Indians of Western Canada. They condemned what they perceived as the violent and disreputable American approach, and believed that, in contrast, their approach, inherited from the British, was just and practical. They argued that there was a duty on the part of the civilized to aid the Indian. The desirable goal for them was agriculture, Christianity, and education. Determination was expressed that Canada, in contrast to the United States, would pursue a policy of fairness and justice, and introduce the peaceful arts of cultivation and husbandry, forging a stable society, rather than one based on continual warfare.

The Métis Resistance of 1869–1870

There was immediate local resistance in Western Canada, centring on the settlement at Red River, by Métis nationalists who resented the intervention of a 'foreign power' and an 'alien authority,' words used in their list of rights. In the

1867 British North America Act a resolution was introduced which would unite Rupert's Land with the new Dominion of Canada. In 1869 the British Parliament passed legislation authorizing the HBC to sell its land to the Canadian government. The HBC profited enormously from this sale, not only immediately, through a payment of £300,000, but through a generous grant of the most fertile and valuable land in the West. All of these arrangements were made without consultation with the residents of Rupert's Land; nor were they informed of the date of the transfer of authority, or the conditions of the transfer. It was conducted simply as a transaction in real estate. Elsewhere in what became Canada, there were protracted debates and votes taken before Canadian Confederation was agreed to, but not in Western Canada. Under the terms of the agreement, the Canadian government agreed to fulfil certain conditions concerning the Indian residents, but almost no mention was made of the Métis, who felt angry and anxious. It was alarming to learn that surveys of the land were to begin in the summer of 1869, even before the actual transfer of authority. The transfer date was moved from 1 October to 1 December as time was required to complete financial arrangements outside of the colony.

The resistance was led by Louis Riel, a young man from a prominent Métis family, who had been educated at Red River and Montreal. In early October, a party of Métis blocked the survey of land south of the Forks. A 'Comité national des Métis' was organized, and a barricade was erected across the road from the settlement to Pembina. The Métis resolved to prevent the newly appointed governor, William McDougall, from crossing the border from Pembina. They occupied Upper Fort Garry, and in November 1869 Riel and his supporters declared themselves to be the colony's provisional government. It was announced that protection of Métis rights was a condition of union with Canada. A plot to overthrow this government, organized and led by prominent men of the 'Canadian Party' at

Red River, was suppressed by the Métis, and forty-eight of them were arrested and imprisoned.

Over the next months there were protracted and diffi-cult negotiations with Canada. The Métis list of rights included provincehood for the region, to be called Assini-boia; representation in the House of Commons and Sen-ate; the right to vote for all males, including Indians, except those in the unsettled areas; bilingual institutions; and denominational schools. On 4 March, one of the pris-oners that the Métis held, Ontarian Thomas Scott, who was charged with insubordination, was executed. Although this event whipped up a frenzy of hatred in Ontario, negotia-tions continued. In the meantime, a military expedition under the command of Colonel Wolseley was dispatched west, fighting mosquitoes and other insects along an over-land route only partially constructed from Thunder Bay, finally 'liberating' Red River towards the end of August 1872. It was raining, there were no welcoming crowds, and they found the gates of Upper Fort Garry open and the place deserted. Although the troops did not, as often claimed, put down the Red River resistance, their presence did amount to the military occupation of the new Canadian province. Some time before the troops arrived, Canada had conceded to a great number of the demands of the Métis. Provincial status was granted, although only a tiny prov-ince, about 260 kilometres square, was created, with the rest of the Northwest to be administered by Ottawa. The Manitoba Act of 1870 provided a constitution for the new province, allowed separate schools, and the use of the French language. One of its terms, section 31, provided for the distribution of 1.4 million acres (567,000 hectares) of public land to the 'Half-Breed' families. The act of 1870 was accepted by the provisional government as the basis for joining Confederation.

There are many interpretations of events in Manitoba in 1869–70. Among the earliest historical writers were men like Alexander McArthur, one of the provisional govern-

ment's prisoners, who went on to become a Winnipeg merchant. He was sympathetic to the Métis and laid the blame
on the blunders made by the Canadian government for not
consulting the Métis and for surveying before the transfer
was complete. Others saw the Métis as hapless puppets in
the hands of devious behind-the-scenes operators. Some
commentators blamed the Roman Catholic clergy for alleg-
edly encouraging the Métis in their misguided apprehen-
sions, and there was also an American conspiracy theory –
that they fomented trouble in order to justify annexation of
the Canadian West. The resistance has been interpreted as
an extension of the struggles and tensions between the
French and the English felt in the older provinces. Stanley
argued, to the contrary, that this was a clash between a
primitive and a civilized people reminiscent of other inevitable confrontations on the frontiers of the Western
world's empire. Stanley did find fault with government
actions, however, and believed the Métis had some sound
reasons for their actions. French historian Marcel Giraud,
who published in 1945, saw the Métis as a backward people
who were unable to cope and adapt; they could not
become agriculturalists and it was inevitable that they
would be doomed under the onslaught of a superior people. In some of his earlier histories, W.L. Morton argued
that the Métis were not a primitive people, that they sought
the civil and political rights of British subjects. He saw the
resistance as the first expression of regional political protest against an insensitive central Canadian government,
typically paying no attention to the wishes of the local residents. Frits Pannekoek has explained the resistance in
terms of the social and political disintegration of Red River
society well before 1869. Racial and religious tension long
pre-dated the arrival of the Canadian Party, according to
Pannekoek. Anglican ministers were largely responsible
for precipitating conflict between the different groups of
Métis. Métis historian Ron Bourgeault has argued that
the Métis reistance was inspired by similar revolutions in

Europe. Riel and others of the burgeoning Métis merchant and working class were inspired by ideals of European liberalism, and wanted responsible self-government, an end to monopoly control of the local economy, access to markets, and freehold land ownership.

Dispersal of the Métis

The controversy that has absorbed scholars lately focuses on the question of what happened to the Métis of Manitoba. After 1870 the Métis began to leave Manitoba in droves. By 1882 they had been allotted less than 600,000 acres (243,000 hectares) of the 1.4 million acres (567,000 hectares) promised, and the rest was diverted to speculators. By 1885 the Métis, once the dominant group, were only 7 per cent of Manitoba's total population. Over 80 per cent of the 'Half-Breed' population in the North-West Territories had left Manitoba, settling in places such as St Laurent at the forks of the Saskatchewan River, at St Antoine-de-Padoue (Batoche), and Prince Albert. Historian D.N. Sprague, originally commissioned by the Manitoba Métis Federation to undertake research, argues that the Canadian government deliberately dispossessed the Métis of their land. There was determination evident well before the events of 1869–70 that the newly acquired territory would become an Ontarian society. The Métis were perceived as a strong military people, and thus a potential threat to profit and to the goal of changing the ethnic face of the province. Central Canadian elites were determined that they would see the Métis dispersed, their strength diminished. Immediate steps were taken to nullify the Manitoba Act, and any political power the Métis might enjoy – only a 'postage stamp' province was created. The government deliberately deprived the Métis of their land, using a variety of strategies, including delay, while the province was flooded with a tide of new settlers who were given every encouragement. Judicial roadblocks were placed in the way of the Métis who wished to get title to their land. On nine occasions between 1872 and 1880, the Department of Justice revised what should have been an unalterable agreement. Meanwhile, the Métis were swamped by a tide of new settlers, and more than 2,000 descendants of original European settlers were dealt a special grant of land each. Sprague concluded that the rights of the Métis were not scrupulously guarded by the government; rather, the goal of the dispossession of the Métis was vigorously pursued.

Based on legal and historical research, Paul L.A.H. Chartrand agreed with Sprague's interpretation, arguing that, in anticipation of massive immigration, the government should have safeguarded the land rights of the Métis, but instead hastened their dispossession and impoverishment. The land-claims agreement that was entrenched in section 31 of the Manitoba Act should be seen, according to Chartrand, as one of the treaties that formalized relations between the Crown and the indigenous people of the West. There should have been a supervised land-settlement scheme of the kind that was intended by section 31. The government failed to implement this scheme, making it virtually impossible to comply with the original object of allowing the Métis to remain in their own places of residence and in their own communities. 'The community was broken up, dispossessed, and displaced,' Chartrand wrote.

The Canadian government retained the services of political scientist Thomas Flanagan and historian Gerhard Ens. In books and numerous articles, they paint a very different picture of these events. Flanagan found evidence that the Métis were fairly, even generously, treated and found no evidence of bad faith on the part of the government. He admits that there were delays in implementing section 31 of the Manitoba Act, but these were unavoidable, and not deliberate – there were more pressing matters to attend to. Mistakes were made, but no one was deliberately hostile towards the Métis. The resistance of 1869–70 was not necessary, as Canada had no intention of depriving the Métis of their rights and their property. Riel and the Métis did a great deal to harm themselves, declaring a provisional government, and then executing Scott. The Métis should not be presented as the hapless victims of the evils of others as this degrades the dignity of individual human beings. The Métis received fair market value for their land, and were not taken advantage of. Gerhard Ens has expanded upon these themes, looking back in time to Métis history before 1869–70 and arguing that the emigration of the Métis from Manitoba began earlier, was closely tied to changes in the economy of the Métis, and was the result of their involvement in the buffalo-robe trade. They expanded out from Red River beginning in the 1850s, taking advantage of new capitalistic opportunities and abandoning their agriculture. The exodus continued until the mid-1870s, when the robe trade collapsed. All of this historical writing has sparked lively debate about what is called by some 'advocacy history,' with concerns raised about whether 'historians for hire' can produce only skewed and one-sided views of the past.

'A Unique and Unenviable Place': Canadian Federal Indian Policy

When the Manitoba and the North-West Territories joined Confederation in 1870, the vast majority of the residents were Aboriginal people, and largely unknown to them, their lives from then on were to be greatly influenced by policies and legislation developed for nearly 100 years in Eastern Canada, and inherited from British imperial practices. The British North America Act of 1867 had given the Canadian federal government jurisdiction over Indians and Indian reserves. In Western Canada, by 1870 there had been over two centuries of European contact, but no formal challenges to Aboriginal land ownership, except within the territory covered by the Selkirk Treaty. The 1870s represents an important watershed for many reasons. The era of efforts to impose the values and institutions of the immigrants or colonists began (although not in earnest until after 1885), and this coincided with the destruction and disappearance of the buffalo economy, just after a devastating epidemic of smallpox and famine. Yet while economic security, independence, and opportunities were to a great extent diminished beginning in the 1870s, Aboriginal people, of course, continued to take action, and make decisions and adopt strategies that influenced the course of events. However, their ability and freedom to control their own lives was increasingly constrained in the last decades of the nineteenth century.

Recent approaches to many of the fundamental documents of Aboriginal and Canadian legal history stress that First Nations were 'not passive objects, but active participants, in [their] formulation and ratification.' To appreciate the meaning of many of these documents then, and the often radically different interpretations of them, it is not enough to have an understanding of the European, written perspective alone. The central policy pursued by the British following the military defeat of the French at Quebec was given expression in the Royal Proclamation of 1763, and this was to form the foundation of the principles governing relations between First Nations and the Crown. The proclamation recognized the 'nations or tribes' of Indians to the west of the British colonies as continuing to own their lands, despite the extension of the new British sovereignty and protection, and directed that the Indians be left undisturbed on these lands. These nations could not sell their lands, however, until they were brought within a colony, and then they could sell only to the Crown, and only through collective and voluntary public action. The proclamation is generally described as a unilateral declaration of the British Crown, but Aboriginal nations played an active role in its genesis, bringing their own considerations, their own power, range of choices, and perspectives, to the agreement. First Nations did not see themselves as dependent, conquered victims of a foreign power, and they proposed peaceful government-to-government relationships of equality, retaining their lands and sovereignty. Different objectives and visions are embedded within the text of the proclamation, and this is why the document is open to differing interpretations.

Beginning in the 1790s, with the arrival of the United Empire Loyalists, the British negotiated treaties with First Nations to permit the expansion of non-Native settlement, generally adhering to the principles established in the Royal Proclamation. At first these were for relatively small parcels of land in exchange for a once-for-all payment. Responsibility for Indian affairs was originally in the hands of a branch of the British military. After the War of 1812, and the decline of the strategic importance of Aboriginal people as military allies, pressure mounted to change the basis of British Indian policy. Missionaries in British North America, as well as a humanitarian lobby in Britain, urged that the Indian Department should take the lead in encouraging Aboriginal people to change their way of life. There was also the example of the United States, where, in the last decade of the eighteenth century, the federal government declared a policy designed to make farmers out of Native Americans, responding to the widely held belief that Native Americans had no choice but to give up their vast tracts of land, with the advantage that they could be taught to farm. From 1828, the British Indian Department sought to foster the creation of self-supporting, as well as self-governing Aboriginal agricultural communities in British North America. In that year the Indian Superintendent of Upper Canada proposed a new function for the department: it would take the lead in 'civilizing' the Indians by encouraging them to settle on reserves, and take up agriculture as a livelihood. Reserves, land set aside for the exclusive use of Indian bands, were now included in the treaties, and the concept of annual payments, or annuities, was introduced. To facilitate the new program, in 1830 in the colonies of Upper and Lower Canada, jurisdiction over the management of Indian affairs shifted from military to civil authorities.

These policies have been assigned 'good marks' by many historians who see in this era the genesis of a humanitarian, benevolent approach to Canada's Aboriginal people. In the British territories, in contrast to the United States (this line of argument goes), there was no hostility, no disposition to eliminate or to coerce; rather, the government played an active role in eliminating reasons for conflict, well in advance of sustained settlement. It is certainly the case that at the same time as the Americans were pursuing the policy of 'removal,' a sizeable portion of the Aboriginal population of the older provinces of Canada remained resident on reserves. Yet there are more cynical views of Britain's 'humanitarian' policy. There was concern about the spread of American 'republican' ideas, and there were good reasons to encourage Aboriginal people to look to Britain as their chief benefactor to gain their loyalty. The concept of reserves and agriculture, which should have ideally allowed Aboriginal people to subsist on a radically reduced land base, permitted a humanitarian veneer to be attached to a policy that was simply aimed at removing an obstacle to non-Aboriginal economic development and settlement.

The direction of the new policy was not entirely unwelcome in the Aboriginal communities. Conscious of the rapid changes unfolding around them, Aboriginal people were not averse to new economic accommodation. With an eye towards preparing themselves to cope with dwindling game and other resources, a number of bands of Upper Canada, even before the adoption of the 'civilizing' program, had used some of the proceeds from land surrenders to fund the establishment of farms and schools with the assistance of missionaries. Aboriginal governments were in favour of agriculture, and the maintenance of the integrity of their society and culture within an agricultural context. For a time beginning in the 1830s there was a progressive partnership in development with Aboriginal governments deciding the degree, nature, and direction of change. They rejected initiatives such as an 1846 effort to introduce the concept of reserve subdivision and individualized property-holding. These councils remained self-governing, with control over their population, land, and finances, until 1860, when responsibility for Indian affairs was transferred from the British government to the government of the United Canadas.

This self-governing status, however, and the progressive partnership, did not last. Colonial legislation of the late 1850s, the transfer of authority over Indian affairs from Britain to the colony, and Confederation radically altered the standing of Aboriginal people. The other parties, groups, or regions that became part of Confederation were consulted and negotiated with, often resulting in contentious and protracted debates. In Canada East, or Quebec, for example, there were concerns about the preservation of their language, religion, culture, and institutions. Aboriginal nations were not consulted, and they were to occupy what historian John Milloy has described as 'a unique and unenviable' place in the new nation. Through the British North America Act, and the legislation aimed at Aboriginal people combined in the comprehensive Indian Act of 1876, the federal government took extensive control of the Aboriginal nations, their land, and their finances. Traditional forms of government were replacd by government/Indian agent–controlled models of government. There was no Aboriginal participation in the formulation and ratification of this legislation; there were protests and objections raised, but these were ignored.

The Indian Act of 1876 incorporated and consolidated earlier legislation of the Assembly of the United Canadas, including the Gradual Civilization Act of 1857 and the Enfranchisement Act of 1869. These acts were based upon the assumption that it was only through individualized property that Aboriginal people could become industrious and self-reliant. With the act of 1857 the Indian Department became an aggressive and disruptive agent of assimilation. It stipulated that any Indian, if he was male, free of debt, literate, and of good moral character, could be awarded full ownership of 50 acres (20 hectares) of reserve land, and would thereby be enfranchised. He would then cut his tribal ties and cease to be an Indian. The goal of full civilization through the enfranchisement of individuals was to be accompanied by the disappearance of Aboriginal communities. In the 1860s there was even more overt encroachment on Aboriginal independence and further destruction of self-government. Enfranchisement had attracted very few qualified candidates, and the tribal governments and their leaders were seen as the obstacles. Self-government had to be abolished. This argument was accepted by the new Canadian government, and the 1869 Enfranchisement Act greatly increased the degree of government control of on-reserve systems. There was to be very little meaningful Aboriginal participation in their own governance. Although chiefs and councillors were to be elected by all male band members over the age of twenty-one, the superintendent general of Indian Affairs decided the time, manner, and place of election, and these officials were to serve at Her Majesty's pleasure, and could be removed by this same official. Band councils were also limited in their areas of jurisdiction, and faced an all-encompassing federal power of disallowance. As historian John Milloy concluded, 'For the original people there was to be no partnership, no degree of home rule to protect and encourage the development of a valued and variant culture, as was the case with French Canada.'

A significant feature of the colonial legislation, later incorporated in the 1876 Indian Act, was the effort to impose Euro-Canadian social organization and cultural values, and English common law, in which the wife was virtually the property of her husband. The act assumed that women were subordinate to males, and derived rights from their husbands or fathers. Women were excluded from voting in band elections and from partaking in band business. They had to prove to government officials that they were of good 'moral' character before they were entitled to receive an inheritance. Beginning with the 1869 act, an Indian woman who married a non-Indian man lost her status as a registered Indian, as did her children. So upon marriage to a non-Indian, the woman would no longer be eligible for residency on reserve land. Even if her non-Indian husband died, her status would not be affected – only remarriage to a status Indian man could reinstate her. On the other hand, white women who married Indian men, and their children, obtained legal status as Indians, and all could reside on reserve land. Another section of the act stipulated that, if an Indian woman married an Indian from another band, she was automatically transferred to the band of her husband, regardless of her personal wishes. This legislation entirely ignored Aboriginal marriage and residency customs, and it was to be keenly resented by women as well as men.

The Indian Act of 1876, which has been described as a 'formidable dossier of repression' and which established race-based laws and limitations in Canada, was originally passed with 100 sections, and this nearly doubled in the next thirty years, to 195. It consigned Aboriginal people to the status of minors; they were British subjects but not citizens, sharing the status of children, felons, and the insane, and it established the federal government as their guardians. Those who came under the act were not allowed to vote in federal or provincial elections, and as they were not voters they were legally prohibited from the professions of law and politics, unless they gave up their Indian status. Through the administration of this act, government agents were able to control minute details of everyday life. There were restrictions on Aboriginal peoples' ability to sell their produce and resources, on their religious freedom and amusements. Many of the clauses of the act were based upon nineteenth-century negative stereotypes of Indians as drunkards, as immoral, as incapable of handling money. The act criminalized for Indians the consumption of alcohol. It also specifically denied Indians rights available even to complete newcomers to the country. It stipulated, for example, that 'no Indian ... shall be held capable of having acquired or of acquiring a homestead ...'

The Numbered Treaties

The First Nations of Western Canada were not informed about this formidable dossier of repression when they entered into treaties in the 1870s. The Indian Act was simply unilaterally imposed, and by not communicating anything about this legislation, government and Crown representatives at treaty negotiations seriously misrepresented the nature of the relationship Aboriginal people were entering into. Aboriginal people were, however, active participants in the treaty negotiations, and the agreements reached reflect the concerns and goals of both sides, although it is now increasingly recognized that these were not fully represented in the written texts of the treaties. There were eight 'numbered treaties' covering the territory of Western Canada (excluding most of British Columbia) made between 1871 and 1899. The written texts of the treaties, prepared well in advance of the sessions, but subject to some change as a result of negotiations, have generally been understood until recently to represent the meaning of these treaties, although that meaning has been open to many interpretations. They have been depicted as just and benevolent instruments through which non-Aboriginal Canada systematically extended its jurisdiction, while offering kindly and generous aid to a population greatly in need of such assistance. The treaties have also been described as tragic misunderstandings, disreputable documents, that were imposed upon a people who had no idea of what was happening. Research that has drawn upon oral history has demonstrated that a focus upon the written text alone projects narrow perceptions of the treaties. The meaning cannot be derived and interpreted from the written words alone as the written texts do not include the Aboriginal understandings. There has also been a Eurocentric tendency to look only at government/and Crown policy and diplomacy with regard to treaty-making, yet Aboriginal societies also had their policy, protocol, ceremonies, and laws. Aboriginal groups had a lengthy history of treaty-making with other First Nations for military, trade, and other purposes. There has been a focus upon the power and authority of the Crown commissioners, but what about the power and authority of the Aboriginal negotiators?

There was significant Aboriginal input with regard to the timing of the treaties, and they were responsible for the introduction of some of the clauses and terms of the agreements. Through treaties Aboriginal people sought to secure not only physical, but cultural survival; to gain assistance in the transition to new economies based on agriculture and husbandry; and to establish peaceful, equitable relations. Canada sought through treaties to acquire legal title to the land in order to complete the transcontinental railway (promised and held out as an enticement to British Columbia in 1871), which would in turn encourage immigration, establish a prosperous economy, and strengthen industry in Eastern Canada. Aboriginal title was to be removed with as little expense as possible, avoiding costly military campaigns. Canadian authorities were also concerned to stop American intrusion north of the forty-ninth parallel, as causes of potential serious international disputes escalated in the 1870s. There were also officials, such as Alexander Morris, who seriously believed that Canadians were honour- and duty-bound to 'elevate' the Aboriginal residents of Western Canada. There was a moral imperative here to export what was perceived as a superior way of life to people assumed to be inferior. It is important to keep in mind that members of a colonizing society can hold powerful convictions that they are behaving altruistically towards the colonized.

Until recently, in written histories the numbered treaties were generally presented as one of the deliberate, orderly, and wise policies pursued by the federal government to ensure the peaceful settlement and prosperous development of the Canadian West. Yet it now seems that there was no particular plan or direction; the pattern and timing of treaty-making, as well as some important clauses, were to a great extent the result of pressure brought to bear by Aboriginal people. In the 1870s Aboriginal people were interested in entering into agreements that could assist them to acquire economic security in the face of a very uncertain future. There was also a great deal of unease and anxiety about the intentions of the government, and concerns were voiced that their land might be taken without consultation. It was learned with alarm that the HBC had 'sold' their land; there had never been any recognition that this company with whom they had traded had any jurisdiction over their land. As legal scholar Sharon Venne recently wrote, 'In present circumstances, it would be tantamount to Pepsi Cola or another such company gaining title to the lands of another country merely by engaging in trading.' Great indignation over the HBC claiming to have sold their land, and then surveying and claiming tracts of land around posts in advance of treaties, was expressed at Treaty Four proceedings: 'A year ago these people [the HBC] drew lines, and measured and marked the lands as their own. Why was this? We own the land; the Manitou [or Great Spirit] gave it to us. There was no bargain; they stole from us ...' Word of troops stationed at Red River in 1870 heightened fears of hostile intentions. The appearance of railway and telegraph surveyors in advance of treaties caused concern. In central Saskatchewan and in Alberta, the NWMP arrived suddenly in advance of treaties and, without permission or consultation, built posts. Pressure for agreements that would provide economic security was brought to bear through messages, deputations to Crown representatives, and interference with survey work.

The numbered treaties appear to be remarkably similar documents. In each of the written treaties, the First Nations agreed to 'cede, release, surrender, and yield up to the Government of Canada for Her Majesty the Queen,' large tracts of land. They were promised, however, that they could continue their vocations of hunting throughout the surrendered tract, except those tracts taken up 'from time to time for settlement.' Reserves of land were to be set aside. (The precise amount of land varied considerably from treaty to treaty. For example, in Treaties Three, Four, and Five, each family of five was allowed one section, or 640 acres [260 hectares], whereas in Treaties One and Two each family was allotted 160 acres [65 hectares].) These reserves were to be administered and dealt with for the residents by the government. Annual payments (varying from five to twelve dollars) were promised to each man, woman, and child, with bigger payments for chiefs and councillors, who were also to receive suitable suits of clothing. They were promised implements, cattle, and seed for the encouragement of agriculture. In Treaties One to Six, the government agreed to maintain schools on reserves, and, in Treaty Seven, to pay the salary of teachers. The signatories solemnly promised to strictly observe the treaty, to conduct and behave themselves as good and loyal subjects of the Queen, to obey and abide by the law, to maintain peace and good order. Closer inspection of the individual treaties, however, reveals significant differences in the circumstances and negotiating tactics of both sides, and in the written and oral accounts of proceedings. There were unique features to each of the agreements, and different understandings of these agreements emerged.

The earliest of the treaties illustrate the concern about future livelihood that was foremost in the minds of Aboriginal spokemen, and the effective negotiating skills of Aboriginal leaders. They also indicate that verbal promises and statements were regarded by Aboriginal people as every bit as binding as those which appeared on the written text. The signatories to the 1871 Treaties One and Two were Saulteaux and the Cree of Manitoba. Their concern about future livelihood was shared by Crown negotiators, who clearly indicated that they wished to encourage an agricultural economy. Alexander Morris, who was the Queen's representative in the treaties made between 1873 and 1876 (Treaties Three to Six), felt that it was Canada's duty to make the new wards self-supporting through agriculture. Initially, however, the Crown negotiators did not intend to provide direct assistance in the transition to an agricultural economy in the way of implements, draught animals, and other necessities of a settled and agricultural lifestyle. In Eastern Canada, agriculture as well as education had received official support and encouragement from government, but specific clauses were not included in treaty terms as obligations upon the Crown. This situation changed in the numbered treaties as a result of the bargaining of Aboriginal negotiators. In Treaty One, specific requests were made for implements, cattle, wagons, and housing. The Crown commissioners orally agreed to this assistance, but the clauses did not appear in the printed versions of Treaties One and Two. Controversy soon surrounded the so-called outside promises, the clauses that related to agricultural assistance, and there was discontent over the non-fulfilment of these terms. These were 'outside' only to the non-Aboriginal negotiators to the treaties; to Aboriginal negotiators, who remembered precisely what had been promised orally, they were an intrinsic part of the treaties. Before the Treaty One negotiations, government surveyor S.J. Dawson had warned his superiors that this would be the case, as 'though they have no means of writing, there are always those present who are charged to keep every word in mind.' Dawson cited the example of an Ojibway principal chief who began an oration by repeating almost word for word what Dawson had said two years earlier. Crown officials agreed to make these a formal part of the treaties in 1875 as a result of the pressure brought to bear by Aboriginal people. The numbered treaties that followed included the terms that provided for agricultural transition in the formal, written treaties.

Treaty Six was made at Fort Carlton and Fort Pitt in 1876 with Plains Cree and Assiniboine. This treaty exemplifies the themes mentioned above; in particular, there was concern about future livelihood. Aboriginal negotiators demanded further clauses that provided for agricultural assistance, and help in making a transition to a new life. As a result of their bargaining, novel terms were added to Treaty Six, including assistance in the event of famine or pestilence, and an additional clause providing for a medicine chest. Reflecting a concern for the future health of their people, the Aboriginal negotiators succeeded in exacting the promise that a medicine chest would be kept at the home of the Indian agent for the use and benefit of the Indians. A troubling aspect of this agreement is that, like Treaty Four, concluded in 1874 at Fort Qu'Appelle with the Cree, Saulteaux, and Assiniboine, a vast number of people, including most of the Cree and prominent leaders, were not informed of the proceedings and were not present. Chief Big Bear, a prominent Plains Cree leader, was not invited by the representatives of the Crown to the original negotiations for Treaty Six.

Studies of Treaty Six that focus upon Aboriginal perspectives reveal fundamentally different understandings of what was agreed to at these proceedings. At the heart of the difference is the certainty that the land was not surrendered, or sold; rather, Aboriginal negotiators agreed to share and to coexist as equals with non-Aboriginals. Given the nature of leadership in Plains societies, and the limits on the powers of the chiefs who entered into treaty, they would not have had the authority to sell or surrender the land. Elders maintain that the land was never sold in the treaty process, and that the wording 'cede, surrender ...' was not included in the original treaty. They accepted the idea that the Queen wanted to make a treaty to share the land with her people, who were in poverty, and the concept of sharing was acceptable. As Harold Cardinal said in an address to Queen Elizabeth II in 1973, 'Our Treaties were agreements between two peoples from different civilizations to share their resources so that each could grow and successfully meet changes brought on by the passage of time.'

Oral histories with the people of Treaty Seven, made in 1877 with the Siksika, Blood, Peigan, Tsuu T'ina, and Nakoda (Stoney) peoples, indicate that a peace treaty was concluded, not a land surrender. They were asked and agreed to put away their weapons, live in peace and harmony, and share the land. But the emphasis on peacemaking was left unrecorded, and instead land surrender was made the most significant part of the written treaty. In the oral record there is no memory of the issue of land surrender being raised and discussed at the proceedings, and no realization that the land was ceded for ever. There is also little trace of the issue being raised in the documentary record of the treaty proceedings. Government officials were anxious to hastily conclude a treaty with the southern Alberta peoples in 1877, and did not want to raise issues such as land surrender as it could well mean that the treaty would be rejected. The Blackfoot were perceived as warlike, volatile, and dangerous as they were well armed. There was concern about potential Blackfoot alliances with the Lakota, who had defeated Colonel George Custer in 1876 and taken up residence in Canadian territory. To the south, in the spring and summer of 1877, there were numerous small battles between the U.S. military and the non-treaty Nez Percé, whose destination was Canada. The making of Treaty Seven coincided with the Nez Percé moving closer and closer to the camp of Sitting Bull, and there was great alarm about the formation of an alliance.

Research into First Nations' perspectives on Treaty Seven has revealed other factors that would have impeded understanding of the concepts embedded in the written document. In Blackfoot there is no equivalent word for 'cede,' and terms such as 'square mile' could not have been translated properly. In Blackfoot there is now a term for mile (*ni'taa'si*), but it entered the language in the early 1900s with the establishment of mission schools, as did the term now used for square (*iksisttoyisi*). There was no word for 'Canada,' only a word for the territory of their own nation. The translators at the proceedings were not competent in all of the Aboriginal languages present, nor could they have understood the Victorian jargon of the commissioners. In the written text of the treaty, there are more than eighty examples of gross misrepresentations of the names of chiefs and headmen signatories, clearly indicating that the translators were not real Blackfoot speakers. The names of Nakoda chiefs, who spoke a Siouan language, were recorded in Cree, indicating that the translator for them, Reverend John McDougall, was not competent in their language.

Conflicting perceptions and interpretations of the treaties are at the root of many contemporary issues. Until recently the treaties have been narrowly interpreted by government and in the courts to mean the words on the written documents. Those who prepared these written documents likely did not fully understand or appreciate what the Aboriginal participants believed they had agreed to. From the government's perspective, treaties were straightforward agreements to secure title to land and resources for settlement and development. First Nations draw attention to the verbal promises and the negotiations, and ask that treaties be understood, not according to the technical meaning of the words, but in the sense that they were understood by Aboriginal people. There must be recognition of the 'spirit' of the treaties, and there should be a flexible and generous interpretation of the terms. The

Supreme Court of Canada has found that courts cannot begin with the assumption that the written text of the treaties manifests a shared communication between the treaty parties. Instead, the courts must take into account the historical context and perception each party might have as to the nature of the undertaking.

An understanding of the spirit of the treaties also requires an appreciation of Aboriginal concepts, philosophies, and ceremonies. It is consistently explained by Elders of the First Nations that the Creator bestowed sacred responsibilites upon them to act as custodians of the land, and that it could therefore not have been possible for them to even consider breaking this inviolable sacred relationship and to cede, surrender, release, and yield up the land. This would be tantamount to giving up their life. According to Harold Cardinal, to the Cree the treaty relationship is rooted in the principles embodied in the term *meyo witchi towin*, meaning 'good, healthy, happy, respectful relationships among equal parties.' The parties agree to act according to the divinely inspired principles of *wak koo too win*, meaning a perpetual relationship patterned after familial concepts. The relationship with the Crown was understood to consist of mutual ongoing sharing arrangements that would guarantee each other's survival and stability. The concept of *wi taski win*, or sharing the blessing of the land in mutual harmony, provided that the sharing arrangements would be fair to each of the parties, enabling both to enjoy the prosperity of the land and *pim atchi hoowin*, or make a living. Through the pipe ceremonies conducted by First Nations when making treaties for the goals of peace and harmony, the most powerful spirits were called upon to assist in maintaining the peace agreement and accompanying commitments of promises. If the agreement was broken, the powerful spirits of the sun, water, thunder, and wind might unleash their wrath upon the attending parties. The serious consequences to breaking vows made to the spirits was a way of ensuring that peace and harmony would be preserved at all costs. The sweet-grass used in the ceremony represented an undertaking between the parties both that their relationship would be non-coercive and that it would be governed according to precepts of honesty, integrity, good faith, gentleness, and generosity. That these ceremonies took place affirms the sacred nature of the agreements and mutual commitments. As Cardinal wrote in his 1969 *The Unjust Society*, 'To the Indians of Canada, the treaties represent an Indian Magna Carta.'

The North-West Mounted Police

The fact that the non-Aboriginal settlement of Western Canada proceeded realtively peacefully, and that 'law and order' was to a great extent observed, has almost entirely to do with the strategies and actions of First Nations. These strategies, outlined above, featured the negotiation of trea-ties in order to ensure that resources would be shared, that independence and integrity would be retained, and that a useful partner in the creation of an enriched way of life would be obtained. Aboriginal negotiators solemnly prom-ised that they would in all respects obey and abide by the law. Even leaders such as Big Bear, who rejected 'taking treaty' for almost a decade, advised and adopted non-confrontational strategies. Despite persistent rumours of Indian 'uprisings' in Western Canada, there were no such events with the exception of Frog Lake (1885; discussed in chapter 7). Promises to maintain peace and good order were observed. Yet credit for the peaceful and orderly set-tlement of the West is generally attributed in written histo-ries to the NWMP, as well as to the treaties, although these are traditionally perceived as entirely a British–Canadian strategy. Both are often presented as essential components of the vision of one man, Prime Minister Sir John A. Mac-donald, who had a grand dream and design for a strong and stable Dominion from sea to sea. While the treaties established the foundation, it was this small force of intrepid few that introduced, and then maintained, law and order, according to many histories of the Canadian West. The force was launched in 1873, and 300 of them, dressed in scarlet to distinguish them from the American cavalry, dressed in blue, made the much-celebrated 'march west' the following year.

A geat deal has been written about the Mounties. There are first-hand accounts, academic as well as popular works of history, fiction, and a 'Heritage Minute.' As historian Keith Walden has written, this vast body of literature has made mythic heroic figures of the Mounties. Most of the accounts contain a heavy cultural bias, as they describe these few men as members of a superior and more power-ful yet humane culture, bringing stability and peace, law and order, to a wild and savage people in a fretful, unin-habitable land. The force is invariably depicted as having forged outstanding relations with Aboriginal people, who welcomed, appreciated, and respected them. They stopped the whisky trade; pacified warlike Indians; and explained the law to them, administering it in equal doses to white and Indian alike. They stood as sterling examples of manly attributes such as integrity, sobriety, and courage.

As Walden observed, none of this is very plausible as few of the residents of Western Canada could possibly have so willingly accepted the intrusion of outsiders into their affairs. There is an element of plausibility, however. The police were welcomed by some leaders and groups. Red Crow, Crowfoot, and other Blackfoot leaders were grateful that the American whisky trade was curtailed. Major James Walsh *did* forge outstanding relations with Sitting Bull and his people when they sought refuge across the border from 1876 to 1881. Yet the Mounties were outsiders intruding into the lives of Aboriginal people, and their actions were not always appreciated. There were indignant reactions to police posts being placed in the path of the buffalo, with-out the government first conferring with them about these establishments. A post such as Fort Calgary was placed at a popular camping and fording site without permission or consultation. As Walter Hildebrandt has argued, the police were sent in the vanguard of a 'new order for the white settlers' to pacify the people in what Prime Minister Macdonald called 'that fretful realm' and make the West a safe place to settle. They were more a military, occupying force than a police force. Their function was to assist in expanding British–Canadian influence, without the costs incurred in costly wars of conquest. They served in a military rather than a police capacity at occasions such as treaty negotiations. At Treaty Seven, the police brought and fired cannons, which the Blackfoot found menacing. As agents of the government they assisted in enforcing the Indian Act and related policies of the Department of the Interior and of Indian Affairs, and soon after their arrival they became vital enforcers of extremely unpopular coercive measures and laws that monitored, controlled, and restrained people. They had powers that were unprecedented in the history of police forces; not only did they introduce and enforce Canadian law, they were also given powers as magistrates and so administered the same laws. Many of the predominantly young men who made up the force were also a far cry from the exemplary models of behaviour that most of the police literature would have us believe, and this caused consternation among Aboriginal leaders. The police indulged in considerable drinking, and brawling among themselves and with the 'citizens.'

Missionary John McDougall was critical of the conduct of the police, whom he found to be fond of whisky, drinking all they could lay their hands on, while supposedly putting down the whisky trade. He also felt that some of the laws and policies the police enforced were foolish and unnecessary. Yet despite his criticisms, McDougall contributed to the 'myth of the Mountie.' In his *Opening the Great West*, McDougall wrote that 'here in the mid-summer of 1875 the fact remained that the major sense of all men in this big

West was to respect the Police and obey the law. Thus without any bloodshed an immense lawless region was being justly and peaceably administered ...' Despite cherished non-Aboriginal origin narratives about Western Canada, the new realm was not, in the last three decades of the nineteenth century, as peaceable as McDougall described, nor was it as lawless as he described in the preceeding years. As in other colonial settings, there was considerable resistance to aspects of the foreign presence that caused colonial authorities grave concern, although there was also accommodation to other aspects. Yet it remains the case that in Western Canada there simply was not the record of continuous violence and conquest that characterized not only the western United States, but many of Britain's imperial enterprises. This had as much to do with the strategies and actions of the Aboriginal residents as with the policies of government and the actions of a handful of police.

7

Ploughing Up the Middle Ground

To Live Together in Common Comfort

Conditions at the start of the era of intensive settlement
could have been favourable to the formation of a common
world, or 'middle ground.' The Manitoba Act was originally intended to allow the Métis to retain their land and
communities in Manitoba, and the treaties established the
terms of accommodation for other Aboriginal people.
There was to have been a sharing of land and resources, for
the mutual benefit of all. The Métis had shown themselves
to be proficient in trade, commerce, politics, as well as agriculture, all of which were central to the new order. Métis
premier of Manitoba John Norquay proudly walked about
the legislature in moccasins. There appeared to be a meeting of minds and aspirations between government and the
people who negotiated the treaties, as both sides professed
an interest in the establishment of farming and ranching
economies. Some Aboriginal women married the newly
arrived males – members of the NWMP, missionaries, and
government officials, including Indian agents and farm
instructors. There is evidence that, in the early years of
intensive settlement, the host Aboriginal people and the
newly arrived settlers learned from and required the assistance of each other. Aboriginal men and women readily
adapted new skills and technology, learning about farming,

cattle-raising, and such tasks as butter-making. The new settlers also drew on Aboriginal knowledge in a wide variety of ways. A Saskatchewan homesteader consulted a man named South Wind when he wanted advice on the best place to locate, and he further learned from him how to use fire to protect stands of timber, and how to replenish the hay swamps. The new settlers relied to a great extent upon 'country provisions' and learned about these resources, such as the fact that the abundant saskatoons were edible, from Aboriginal people. A great many of the new settler women relied on Aboriginal midwives, and more generally upon the knowledge women had of the medicinal value of plants.

There was potential then for a middle ground, and there were both Aboriginal and non-Aboriginal people who aspired to this goal in the 1870s. Journalist F.L. Hunt, who was married to a Cree woman, was present at the Treaty Four negotiations in 1874, and he expressed his wish in an 1876 article that people could live together in 'common comfort.' Hunt wrote, 'I am greatly moved when I seek to gather in the scope of the splendid future of this country – its capacity for an enduring greatness, its strength to feed and to care.' He called upon Canadians to remember that 'it is not merely to the tolerance of the Indians [that Canada] ... owes its present safety, but also to their sheltering aid and care.' He pointed out that the Indians had protected, clothed, and sustained the newcomers in the past. Hunt concluded that 'the escutcheon of Manitoba today should be an Indian succouring a suppliant white man, and, in keeping with their voiceless benefits, upon every faithful heart let it be written: "*We do not forget.*"'

Crop of Broken Promises

Hunt was soon disappointed in his wish that people could live together in common comfort. He briefly took a job as a farm instructor but found he could not bear the distress

and starvation that surrounded him, and he feared the consequences of such suffering. In parts of the West that did
not experience rapid intensive settlement, there persisted
signs of operation on a middle ground, but in the more
southerly 'settlement belt,' there was not to be a common world of sharing and mutual accommodation. Relations between Aboriginal people and government became
quickly strained as promises were not kept, and great hard-
ship resulted. For their part government officials projected
the idea that Aboriginal people were unable to cope with
change, that they desperately and stubbornly clung to the
'old' ways, and that their spokesmen could be dismissed
as chronic complainers. Rigid boundaries were created
between the new arrivals and the host Aboriginal population, physically, socially, and mentally. In setting up their
communities the new arrivals rejected social and economic
interaction. In the years immediately after the treaties, government support for the establishment of reserve economies was not adequate. There was an erosion in the spirit
of amity and *entente* with which the venture might have
been more successfully broached. The gulf of understanding deepened, as people began to regard each other with
distrust and aversion. Aboriginal people had reason to feel
that they had been deceived, and led along a path that had
ended in betrayal. They were getting the clear impression
that the treaties were viewed cynically by the government as
a means of getting peaceable possession of the country
without any regard for their welfare. Discontent was heightened in the early 1880s, when government measures aimed
at economizing led to further hunger and distress. There
were several incidents of assault upon farm instructors, who
were generally the officials in charge of rationing, and
Indian agency storehouses were broken into. A study of the
post-treaty years challenges comfortable assumptions about
Canada's benevolent and wise Indian policy, as the history
is one of broken treaty promises, fraud, and the use of
coercive measures, enforced with the aid of police and

later troops. As efforts were made to tighten control, tension and resentment mounted, and by 1885 there was a volatile situation in many parts of the Northwest.

Those who attempted to begin farming in the immediate post-treaty era were met with many frustrations. It was clear from the treaty negotiations and before that many Aboriginal people were interested in the establishment of farming and/or ranching economies (although not all wished to pursue these opportunities). It is a widely held misconception among non-Aboriginal people that the original Plains people were not at all interested in agriculture, and did not have the capability to farm. Historians have been influential in re-inforcing this view, adopting uncritically the favoured explanation of government officials and elected representatives of the late nineteenth and early twentieth centuries, who belittled and deprecated the abilities of Aboriginal farmers in order to absolve the department of any responsibility for the failure of agriculture. Similarly, Aboriginal women were anxious to learn the skills and adopt the technology that would permit them to participate in the new economy. These efforts, too, were stymied by a lack of tools, ingredients, and supplies. Butter making, loaf bread, knitting, all required equipment that was beyond the means of most. In official publications, however, these women were blamed for the slum conditions and poor health that characterized reserve life.

In *The Birth of Western Canada*, G.F.G. Stanley argued that Plains people cherished traditions that made them notoriously poor farmers and stockmen. They were unable to adapt to new conditions of life such as farming, which was regarded as 'tedious' to those used to the thrill of the buffalo hunt. According to Stanley, government officials eventually persuaded them that their only hope for the future lay with agriculture on the reserves, but their character and tradition militated against any advances in farming. Stanley's interpretation reflected widely held beliefs that Aboriginal societies were tradition-bound, static, and incapable of change and innovation. My own study, *Lost Harvests*, which built upon earlier work by Noel Dyck and John Tobias, challenged interpretations such as Stanley's. Plains people were clearly interested in establishing farming and ranching economies, displaying greater resolution and determination to see farming succeed than did government administrators. Self-supporting agricultural communities were not established by 1900, but this had to do with government Indian Affairs policies, combined with other adversities and misfortunes shared by all other Western farmers. It was not cultural attributes that prevented them from farming successfully.

Despite concerted efforts on the part of Aboriginal workers, farming proved nearly impossible in the early reserve years. The implements and livestock promised in the treaties were inadequate. Large groups of up to fifty families were expected, for example, to share one yoke of oxen, at a time when a team was required by every farming family to begin earning a living from the soil. In addition to the overall inadequacy of the assistance promised in the treaties, government officials were reluctant and tentative about distributing what was promised. The people prepared to farm expected their supply of implements, cattle and seed immediately, but officials were determined to adhere strictly to the exact wording of the treaties which stipulated that these items were not to be distributed until people were settled on their reserves and cultivating. They could not cultivate until they had implements to break the land, yet these were not to be distributed until they were settled and cultivating. Some government officials believed that distributing any of these promised items encouraged 'idleness.' The assistance solemnly promised under the terms of the treaties was viewed by non-Natives as gifts or charity.

There were problems with the quality and distribution of seed grain. Seed arrived in a damaged state, or was received when it was far too late to sow. It was also impossible for people to congregate to seed in the spring without assistance in the way of provisions. The people of Treaty Six had successfully bargained for this, but there was no such provision for Treaty Four people, and it proved impossible for more than a very few to remain on their reserves and work when there was nothing to live on. Aboriginal farmers were also hampered by the kind of ploughs that they were issued, which were not suitable to Western soil conditions. Much of the equipment and livestock supplied by contractors under the terms of the treaties was not only scandalously inferior, but in some cases completely unfit for use. An 1878 commission of investigation confirmed that it was standard practice to furnish the Indian Department with 'the most inferior articles,' and Indian commissioner J.A.N. Provencher was found guilty of fraud in the awarding of contracts. Some of the goods and stock were simply refused by the treaty people. Wild Montana cattle were sent to many reserves in the late 1870s. These beasts were unaccustomed to work, and could not be hitched to a plough. Treaty Six bands were astounded when these cattle were brought to them from Montana, when tame cattle could have been purchased at Prince Albert or Red River. Most of the wild cattle died over the first winter of 1878–9. As one Plains Cree chief stated, 'We know why these Montana cattle were given us; because they were cheaper, and the Government, thinking us a simple people, thought we would take them.' He was correct in this, as it became clear during the 1878 investigation that individuals in Winnipeg had profited by purchasing these creatures from Montana at about half the rate that they actually charged the Indian Department, pocketing a substantial profit.

Aboriginal farmers laboured under other disadvantages as well. In the early years there were no grist mills located near reserves, and the wheat they raised was of no use to them without milling facilities. With the disappearance of the buffalo, their main source for most of their apparel also vanished. They lacked clothing and footwear, which one official described as the greatest drawback to their work. To make moccasins, they cut up old skin lodges, but the avail-ability of these, too, rapidly diminished. Often hungry, weak, and ill, people could not work no matter how willing. There was little progress in agriculture on most reserves in the years immediately after the treaties were signed. Early on, government officials began to insist that this had to do with the indifference and apathy of the people, who rejected farming, and inflexibly and stubbornly insisted on pursuing hunting and gathering. Newcomers seemed to readily adopt and to project these views as well. Anger and jealousy focused on the assistance which treaty people received, assistance which was mistakenly perceived as gifts, as charity, and as unfair to the new arrivals, who regarded themselves as the 'true' settlers.

Newcomers enjoyed greater economic opportunity, priv-ileges, and freedom. Journalist F.L. Hunt wrote in 1876 that 'to those, and there are many, who view with dissatisfaction anything at all being given to the Indians, it may be a con-solation to know that he would be much better off as a Mennonite or Dane than as a Cree or Otchipwe.' Under many of the treaties, they were allocated less land, 1 square mile or 128 acres (52 hectares) per family of five, in con-trast to the 160 acres (65 hectares) allowed the individual male homesteader. Newcomers had the option of leaving poor land, or land that was distant from transportation and markets, and try their luck elsewhere. Reserve residents had little choice but to persevere, as under the Indian Act they were excluded from taking homesteads. Newcomers had many opportunities to expand their holdings, while reserve farmers had no such options. Opportunities for land acquisition available to the new arrivals included the free homestead of one-quarter section, and at various times the right of pre-emption on an additional quarter-section, the right to make a second homestead entry, expansion through family expansion, and purchase, including provi-sion for a purchased homestead. Indian reserve farmers could not obtain loans, because they were not regarded as the actual owners of any property, however extensive and valuable their improvements might be, and they had difficulty obtaining credit from merchants. Because of many technicalities and prohibitions of the Indian Act, Indians were prevented from doing business or transacting even the most ordinary daily affair. People who came under the Indian Act were prevented by a permit system from selling, exchanging, bartering, or giving away any produce grown on their reserves without the permission of a government official. The most recent arrivals to the country had far more rights, privileges, and freedoms than the original inhabitants.

Home Farm Experiment

Just at the end of the 1870s, alarming reports from the Northwest of starvation and destitution galvanized Ottawa officials into taking action. The result was a hastily contrived scheme which was intended to both feed and instruct reserve residents. A squad of farm instructors, mainly from Ontario, was assembled and dispatched west in the summer of 1879. They were to establish 'home farms' at fifteen sites in the Northwest. These did not include northern sites, or any in Manitoba, but were located among the Plains people, who were formerly dependent on the buffalo. The instructors were to raise large quantities of provisions to support not only themselves, their families, and their employees, but also the neighbouring Aboriginal population. They were also to establish model farms, and spend time assisting reserve farmers in all of their operations, including building houses and outbuildings.

The plan was poorly conceived. Most of the instructors were unfamiliar with conditions in the West, and knew nothing about Aboriginal people. They had to be provided with both guides and interpreters. They were chosen from a patronage list by the prime minister himself. But the tasks assigned the instructors were beyond the resources and capabilities of any individual, however well acquainted he might be with conditions and the people. It soon proved that the instructors had difficulty establishing even the most modest farms. They seldom visited the reserves, and lacked even basic knowledge about the people they were to instruct. The program proved to be an administrative nightmare, and was characterized by scandal, resignations, and dismissals. It also invited much comment from the Opposition benches, and it became an object of scorn, indignation, and bemusement. By 1884, the department had officially retired the policy, which had already undergone much modification.

The home-farm program, however flawed, and the assignment of farm instructors did indicate important government commitment to the establishment of farming economies on reserves in Western Canada. Yet an immediate result of the program was to further generate anger and resentment among the newly arrived settlers, and the eventual giving-in to these critics undermined government commitment. Non-Aboriginal residents viewed the program as unfair, because so much appeared to be done to assist Aboriginal farmers. The home-farm program ingrained the idea that Aboriginal farmers were being lavishly provided with farm equipment and other assistance. They were even given some rations, which many non-Aboriginal newcomers viewed as a reward for idleness, and as unfair. Besides, it was popularly thought, all of this was a waste of money as Indians were incapable of farming.

There remained a situation of grim destitution on most reserves into the early years of the 1880s. Appalling conditions prevailed, for example, in the Touchwood Hills of Saskatchewan in the winter of 1883–4, where their crop was destroyed by frost, and hunting was also a failure. People were without footwear and clothing, and it was a bitterly cold winter, with a heavy snowfall. There was no hide even to make the nooses for rabbit snares. It was reported that the people were very much downcast, and afraid that they were going to starve. In the midst of this bitterly cold winter, major cutbacks in funding were announced, which meant dramatic reductions in rationing on reserves. Decisions such as these were made by bureaucrats in Ottawa, in this case Deputy Superintendent General Lawrence Vankoughnet. He had little direct experience with the people and conditions in the West, and was governed by a passion for petty economy. These rations were inadequate for subsistence; as Maureen Lux has argued in a recent study of the health of First Nations in Western Canada, state prisoners in Siberia were given more than twice the rations allotted on Treaty Four reserves in 1884. This policy of reduction in rations resulted in several instances of collective action to take food in the reserve storehouses. The government authorities viewed this as theft, but reserve residents maintained that what was in the storehouses belonged to them, and in helping themselves they were taking only what was theirs. They justified such action on the grounds that they were starving, and that as their request for food was refused, they had no choice but to help themselves. In some cases such action was also accompanied by assaults upon farm instructors, who were in charge of rationing and the storehouses. The failure of the government to effectively assist in the establishment of viable reserve economies, and the realization of the worst fears of the Aboriginal leaders who made the treaties resulted in concerted protests and efforts to assert their rights. A tradition of protest against unfulfilled treaty promises, and other policies that limited economic and cultural freedom began immediately after the treaties were made.

Big Bear and the Campaign for Cree Consolidation

The actions and strategies of Aboriginal people in the post-treaty era were varied and complex. Plains Cree chief Big Bear represents one strategy. His reputation has been badly maligned during his lifetime and since. He was cast as a symbol of Aboriginal backwardness, as intransigent, cantankerous, surly, and obstructive, as were other Aboriginal leaders who protested and resisted. These negative images were reinforced during the months of the 1885 North-West Resistance when he was held in the non-Aboriginal public imagination as the person responsible for the deaths of nine men at Frog Lake, and for putting two white women widowed by these events through a horrible ordeal. Big Bear came to symbolize the warlike savage, who would have to be eliminated in order that proper white civilization could proceed undisturbed.

This portrait of Big Bear as dangerous and devious has been significantly altered and revised in more recent studies that depict him as an astute defender of his people and as one of the most influential leaders in a Cree diplomatic campaign for autonomy, solidarity, and treaty rights in the decade before 1885. Born near Jackfish Lake, north of the Battlefords, in the 1820s of Ojibway and Cree heritage, Big Bear earned great respect among his own people for his political acumen, as well as for his religious and medical wisdom. He was associated with the bear spirit, was the holder of a bear bundle, and of a sacred medicine pipe. By the later 1870s, Big Bear was at the height of his power and influence, with a massive following of 400 lodges (approximately 2,000). Yet he was not invited to the negotiations for Treaty Six; no effort was made to inform him or Little Pine, another influential Cree leader. Big Bear, who arrived at Fort Pitt two days after business had been completed, then had the option of signing, and he was later given the opportunity to sign an adhesion to the treaty, but he refused. He was concerned that the treaties would destroy Cree autonomy and he was also convinced that they did not contain adequate terms. According to Hugh Dempsey, Big Bear was well aware that the government had agreed to alter Treaties One and Two as a result of pressure from the Aboriginal people of Manitoba, and he believed the government would do so again if only the Cree could speak with a unified voice. He opted not to sign, and to allow the government a period of probation in which to honour the commitments already made.

Big Bear and his followers spent time in the United States following the remaining herds, but by the early 1880s they were among 4,000 who congregated in starving condition near Fort Walsh in the Cypress Hills. Big Bear saw and heard evidence of the failure of the government to live up to treaty promises. He hoped that a large Cree territory could be created in the Cypress Hills, where they could remain united and independent. Government officials were opposed to the idea of a Cree territory for the same reasons that the Cree favoured it; it was feared that the residents would remain autonomous and would be impossible to control. The Cree and Assiniboine were not allowed to settle in the Cypress Hills, despite the fact that several bands chose this site, and reserves were surveyed. This action was a violation of treaty promises, and subsequent government promises that the people could choose the location of their reserves.

In the early 1880s government officials of the Indian Department, with the assistance of the NWMP, used the withholding of rations as a tool to bring people to submission. To factilitate the removal of people from the Cypress Hills in 1882, Fort Walsh was closed. Big Bear and his followers were slowly and deliberately starved into submission at Fort Walsh, as they received no assistance until they agreed to take treaty. The chief's influence began to wane, and his group of followers to splinter. Indian commissioner Edgar Dewdney announced that he would recognize any adult male Cree as chief of a new band if that man could induce 100 or more persons to accept him as leader. Dewdney expected that the 'recalcitrant' leaders would be deserted. Almost half of Big Bear's band joined Lucky Man or Thunderchild to form new bands in order to receive rations. Faced with anger and impatience, even from his own family, Big Bear had no choice but to accept the treaty. They moved to the Frog Lake district, where a reserve site was under negotiation. The chief refused to finally select a reserve as he saw this as his last negotiating point. He and other Cree leaders also wished to have a concentrated Cree territory in the north near the Battlefords. But Big Bear's followers split into factions, and his supporters continued to steadily erode as rations were withheld, and suffering was acute.

A central strategy of Cree leaders at this point, including Big Bear, Little Pine, and Piapot, was to consolidate the Cree through a grand council, and through the concentration of their people further to the north. Efforts were made to seek Blackfoot support for the movements, and attempts were made to bring leaders together in council. Piapot's effort to do so in Treaty Four was met by government threats to cut off rations, to arrest Piapot, and to depose any chiefs who met with him. Big Bear was successful, however, in organizing a thirst dance and council at Poundmaker's reserve near the Battlefords in June 1884. The movement for Cree consolidation seemed to be gaining momentum. At an 1884 council of Cree leaders of the Carlton District, a detailed list of treaty violations for which the Cree demanded redress was drawn up. They felt deceived by 'sweet promises,' and stated that, unless their grievances were remedied by the summer of 1885, they would take whatever measures were necessary, short of war, to get redress.

These events alarmed government authorities, and much of the blame was assigned to Big Bear, who continued to earn the reputation of being an obstreperous, even dangerous, troublemaker, who led a gullible and misguided people. His diplomatic career and campaign on behalf of the Cree ended abruptly in April 1885 during brief minutes of violence at Frog Lake that left nine men dead, including the Indian agent, farm instructor, and two priests. Big Bear was powerless to prevent the events at Frog

Lake, and he had no responsibility for them. He used what influence he retained to help protect the prisoners and ensure that the troubles did not worsen, and he also offered protection to the 'civilians' of Fort Pitt, who decided it was safer for them to join with this group of Cree. After the Métis were defeated at Batoche in May 1885, the focus of the North-West Campaign (discussed in detail in chapter 8) came to focus upon the pursuit of Big Bear, who was never caught, but gave himself up in July. Despite his lack of responsibility and his efforts to promote peace, Big Bear was tried and found guilty of treason-felony. During the months of the pursuit he was depicted as an arch-criminal. After his conviction, he served time in jail until he was released in 1887, his health and spirit broken. As historian John Tobias has argued, the Riel Resistance of 1885 provided government authorities with a new instrument with which to make the coercive policy effective, and the troops, as well as subsequent measures of surveillance and control, were used to destroy the Cree movement for an Indian territory.

Sitting Bull in Canada

The Lakota (or Teton Sioux) for many years successfully pursued a strategy of military resistance against American imperialism, a military resistance that has no parallel in the territory that became Canada. The Lakota were an expansive and powerful military society who gained control of much of the Northern Plains together with their Arapaho and Cheyenne allies. They were engaged in warfare with other Plains groups, the Crow and the Pawnee, and they were also a formidable military challenge to the American army, which proved incapable of subduing them for over twenty years. The Lakota scored a significant military victory at the 1876 Battle of Little Bighorn in Montana, where General George A. Custer met his end along with the defeat of the Seventh Cavalry. It was a great victory, but it also meant the end of their strategy of military resistance, as they experienced rapid dispossession and marginality. The American military amassed an army of 4,000 men to continue the campaign, and in the depth of the winter of 1876–7 with the U.S. military ruthlessly pursuing them, they scattered into small bands. Some groups surrendered, but a number of bands crossed the line into Canada. In all, about 2,000 Lakota crossed the Chanku Wakan, or forty-ninth parallel, into Canada to Wood Mountain.

They were not the first of the Sioux to seek refuge in British territory. Following the Minnesota Uprising of 1862, a number of Dakota bands fled north for security. Dr Charles A. Eastman's book *Indian Boyhood* described the years when his family and people took refuge in Manitoba. The Dakota asked to remain permanently, spoke to authorities about their ancient history of northern origins, and displayed the medals that their fathers received from King George for faithfully serving the British during the War of 1812. They recalled that pledges of protection had been given to them, and also claimed the right to be on British soil. The Dakota were granted reserves in Manitoba and Saskatchewan, and the Lakota hoped for similar treatment. The Lakota informed the superintendent of the NWMP at Fort Walsh, J.M. Walsh, that they wanted refuge, that they feared for the lives of the women and children, and that they were tired of being hunted. They did not cross the line because they had heard of the sterling reputation of the 'Redcoats'; suspicion and tension clouded many of the initial encounters between the NWMP and the Lakota, who feared that they might act in concert with the U.S. army. Eventually Walsh did win the trust of the refugees and earned a reputation as a fair-minded policeman. Sitting Bull pledged that he would do no more fighting, and observe the law, and Walsh then agreed to supply them with enough ammunition to hunt for food, although they were told that they would not be granted reserves and had to return across the line.

The presence of the Lakota created a host of problems and tensions. They were enemies of the people of the Northern Plains, and competition over dwindling buffalo could strain relations further. There was a contradictory concern that Sitting Bull might become a magnet for other disaffected Aboriginal Plains leaders, potentially forming a strong military opposition centred in the Wood Mountain/ Cypress Hills district. There was fear that many more Lakota and other groups might move north, and this was to some extent confirmed in 1877, when about 100 Nez Percé refugees arrived from across the line, many of them wounded as a result of being hounded by the American military, with whom they had engaged in battle at several places in Montana that year. Canadian authorities were concerned that Canada might be used as a base from which to mount attacks into the United States. American authorities asked for the unconditional surrender of the Lakota, which meant that they would have to give up their horses and guns, but it was also hoped that Canada would keep the refugees and create reserves for them. Canada consistently refused to do so, and the United States insisted that the Lakota were now Canadian Indians.

By the spring of 1878, there were about 5,000 Lakota in Canadian territory. Diplomatic relations between the two nations were further strained when some of the Lakota hunted and camped, but also raided south of the border. That summer, fires lit just south of the forty-ninth parallel burned off the grass so that the buffalo were unable to move into Canadian territory. Sitting Bull himself was south of the border in 1879 when he was attacked by troops under the command of General Nelson Miles. Canadian authorities became determined to remove the Lakota, and once again the weapon of starvation was used. Assistance in the way of supplies of food and ammunition were promised, but only if they would leave. Disease and destitution plagued the Lakota, and in small groups they began to return to the United States. Walsh was replaced by Superintendent L.N.F. Crozier, who did not work towards the establishment of amicable relations. Authorities apparently felt that Walsh had become too friendly with the Lakota and that this had compromised his ability to carry out his orders. Walsh believed that the Lakota were shamefully abused by the American government. In the summer of 1881, with his people in a state of desperation, Sitting Bull agreed to accept the food and supplies that could tide them over during the trip to Fort Buford Dakota, and they left Canada.

Canadians have long prided themselves on the story of the friendship and mutual respect that grew between the NWMP and the Lakota, yet historians Walter Hildebrandt and Brian Hubner have argued that it was instead a regretable and shameful episode, a friendship betrayed. The Lakota could have been granted asylum as the one-time allies of the British, instead of forcing them, through the tool of starvation, to return to the mercy of the authorities they despised. A few Lakota remained in Canada, and in 1909 they were granted a reserve at Wood Mountain.

Removal of the Assiniboine from the Cypress Hills

The experiences of the Assiniboine are often overlooked in histories of the post-treaty era in Western Canada. Their story, along with that of the coercive policies applied to the Cree, challenges images of an honourable and benevolent Canadian government. Canada, too, had its incidents of 'Indian Removal.' The Assiniboine bands of Long Lodge and Man Who Took the Coat wished to take reserves in the Cypress Hills, a place that was spiritually and economically important to them, and in 1880 a reserve of 340 square miles (880 square kilometres) was surveyed for them. They were assigned a farm instructor, and their early efforts at agriculture were reasonably successful. Despite the initial promise of this reserve location, and the desire of the Assiniboine to remain in the Cypress Hills, the government adopted measures to enforce their removal from this area. Initially efforts were made to induce the Assiniboine to remove themselves voluntarily to take up reserves in the southeastern corner of present-day Saskatchewan, but they refused to cooperate with the attempts to relocate them. There were at least five instances of efforts being made to induce them to leave the Cypress Hills. After the fifth occasion, in February 1882, the Indian agent wrote that they wanted to remain permanently in the Cypress Hills: 'Their chief arguments against moving were that they were brought up in this country, that although they had given their country to the Queen who had promised them a Reserve in whatever part of the country they liked to pick out, that they did not like the northern country or the Indians living there and hoped that the Government would allow them to remain here.' Government tactics to enforce removal included the announcements that farming in the Cypress Hills was a failure, and that the Assiniboine were willing to leave voluntarily to a new reserve south of Indian Head. Rations were reduced, so that by 1882 people were in a desperate state. Colonel A.G. Irvine of the NWMP wrote in May of that year that 'I have fully determined to starve them out if they remain here.' Dewdney's instructions to Irvine were that people of the Cypress Hills should be told that they had brought suffering upon themselves, and that 'the longer they continue to act against the wishes of the Government, the more wretched will they become.'

Assiniboine elders relate that they were removed against their will, and that they faced appalling conditions during this removal in the spring of 1882. Dan Kennedy wrote that 'we left Cypress Hills, our favourite hunting territory – the land of the evergreens, chinook winds, and running brooks – and moved to our reserve, the Skull Mountainettes – the land of the dead – where two epidemics of smallpox wiped out two large tribes of Crees in the forties of the last century.' They were provided only minimal rations, and did not have proper transportation. Many who made the journey were severely weakened, and several died along the route to Indian Head. They did not favour their new location at Indian Head, where they had a reserve that was much smaller than the one in the Cypress Hills. The location of their new reserve was Win-cha-pa-ghen, or Skull Mountainettes, as the hills were littered with skulls. There was an alarming amount of sickness, as a result of change in diet from fresh meat to bacon. A number of Assiniboine returned to the Cypress Hills in August 1882. Here they spent a winter under deplorable conditions. Surgeon Augustus Jukes of the NWMP reported they 'are literally in a starving condition and destitute of the commonest necessaries of life ... it would be difficult to exaggerate their extreme wretchedness and need.' He warned that, without immediate action, the consequences would be 'disastrous and even appalling.' The following spring, the Assiniboine, in terrible physical condition, were brought to Maple Creek, and loaded onto railway flatcars. Barely *en route*, the flatcars overturned, and the accident injured a number of people. They then refused to ride the train any further, and walked the remaining more than 400 miles (640 kilometres) to Indian Head. A number of them died along the way.

8

Turning Point: 1885 and After

Confrontation of 1885

The year 1885 is an important turning point in Canadian history. Historian Jack Bumsted has argued that it might be a far more appropriate watershed than 1867, which politically brought together the older colonies of Canada. In 1885 the railway across Canada was completed, stitching the country together as never before. Yet, that same year, the nation was divided as never before in its young life by the controversy that emerged between French- and English-speaking Canadians over the issue of Louis Riel, establishing a central tension that would from then on characterize Canadian life. It was also an important turning point for the people of Western Canada, as it finally put to rest any hopes or possibilities for a progressive partnership, for a shared or common world, and cemented the tension and distance between Aboriginal and non-Aboriginal that has also been a characteristic of the history of Canada. Riel brought the issues of Aboriginal and French-Canadian rights together in 1885, and curiously they remain together in many ways today, as Riel is once again in the news and Canadians debate the right of a minority to take separate action against what they perceive to be an intransigent and insensitive central government.

The events of 1885, and the causes leading to these

events, remain topics of great controversy among historians, and the general public, and a vast literature has been produced. Widely different interpretations emerge from the pens (now computers) of historians, depending on how evidence is emphasized and sometimes ignored or overlooked. New perspectives, evidence, and interpretations are continually being added. There is such little agreement that it is difficult to even provide an overview of the basic 'facts.' There is not even agreement over the issue of what to call the events of 1885 – resistance or rebellion. The term 'resistance' is now widely accepted for the events of 1869–70 in Manitoba, as it is agreed that there was a vacuum of authority at the time of the declaration of the provisional government, thus no government to 'rebel' against. 'Rebellion' is regarded by many as appropriate for the events of 1885, as Canada possessed an internationally recognized title to the Northwest at the time of the declaration of the provisional government. Others resent 'rebellion' altogether as it suggests that Métis grievances and actions were not legitimate.

Any account of 1885 must begin with the concerns of the Métis, who had established settlements at various sites in Western Canada, including those at St Laurent and Batoche. The Métis greatly outnumbered the whites in the Territories, and at their settlements along the South Saskatchewan they had river-lot farms, churches, mills, stores, and ferries. During the 1870s, as the federal government moved to assert control over the Northwest, the Métis were increasingly concerned that little was being done to recognize their prior rights. In the decade when the numbered treaties were being made, nothing was done to 'treat' with the Métis. For the Métis as well as the Indians, the disappearance of the buffalo meant that their means of subsistence was undermined, and there were concerns about future security. The fortunes of even the wealthier Métis merchants, freighters, and farmers were to a great extent dependent on the bufalo. The new technologies of steamboats and the railway meant a loss of sources of income, such as freighting.

It was the question of land that came to dominate discussions among the Métis of St Laurent and surrounding settlements. They wanted the lands they occupied surveyed and patents granted. They wanted their river lots surveyed and wanted Ottawa to permit this irregularity in the grid survey. They also wished to have the same sort of assistance with agriculture granted to those who signed the treaties – seed grain, and implements. (A number of those who took treaty were in fact Métis, and close relatives of those in the Métis settlements, but they chose to be identified as Indians.) There was also concern about the issue of representation on the North-West Council, and about measures to protect the buffalo. As newly arrived settlers began to surround them, the Métis legally remained squatters with no title to their land. Meanwhile, the Canadian Pacific Railway (CPR) and the Hudson's Bay Company (HBC) were being granted enormous parcels of land in what was regarded as the fertile belt. The Métis forwarded petitions, and there were many other words of warning and advice from missionaries, surveyors, policemen, and casual travellers who urged that the Métis land question be dealt with without delay. Initially the Métis received support and sympathy from non-Aboriginal settlers, who were also frustrated in their dealings with the distant federal government. Those who had settled along the proposed northerly route of the CPR were particulary angry in the early 1880s that the transcontinental had been rerouted many miles to the south.

These warnings were not heeded, and the question of why is at the heart of much of the debate over the causes of the confrontation. It was the Conservative government under Prime Minister John A. Macdonald, back in power in 1878, that failed to heed the warnings and take action. Under the Dominion Lands Act of 1878, the Canadian government was given the authority to make an arrangement that would satisfy the Métis. Yet no such action was taken, and it cannot be argued that this was because of a lack of information. Perhaps Macdonald was too preoccupied with other affairs; he was trying to complete the massive and expensive railway project, and he needed to persuade Parliament that it was worth several more million dollars. Perhaps Macdonald simply did not foresee that events in the West could lead to such a grave situation. Yet the prime minister had experience with an earlier Métis resistance. As G.F.G. Stanley wrote, 'There may have been excuses for Sir John A. Macdonald in 1869; there were none in 1885.' Doug Sprague has argued that the government delays were deliberate, that this was a studied neglect because Macdonald sought an exploitable crisis in the far western reaches of the Dominion in order to persuade Parliament of the need to hastily complete the faltering railway, and that he further aspired to provoke Riel into declaring another provisional government in order that he could be charged with treason. The immediate and massive military response to the events in the Northwest is generally depicted in our histories as perfectly logical, as inevitable, but why the scale of the response? In many ways this was out of all proportion to the minor rioting that had happened. Thomas Flanagan, by contrast, has argued that the Canadian government was on the verge of responding when the confrontation began; the Métis were to be allowed to qualify as homesteaders within the sectional survey. The actions of the Métis were not at all justified, according to Flanagan, as the government aimed for true conciliation. There was no concerted campaign to destroy the Métis or to deprive them of their rights; mistakes were made, but these were honest mistakes. Flanagan assigns much of the blame for the confrontation to Riel alone, who he believes was pursuing personal objectives.

In 1884 a delegation of four Saskatchewan Métis persuaded Louis Riel to return with them and assist in their campaign for rights. Riel was then living in Montana; he was an American citizen, a schoolteacher, and he had married. Since 1870, Riel had three times been elected for a Manitoba constituency, but he was expelled from the House. In 1875 he was offered an amnesty, conditional upon exile from Canada for five years. He travelled, and he spent about two years in asylums in Quebec. Riel's letters written during his confinement reveal that he claimed to be receiving divine revelations; he saw himself as a prophet of the New World, endowed by God to renew religious faith in North America, and he saw the Métis as a Chosen People. Riel's period of banishment was long past in 1884, and he accepted the invitation to return to Canada, and once again lead his people. In Saskatchewan he was initially favourably received by Métis and non-Aboriginal alike. He addressed meetings of new settlers and Métis, and he impressed all with this moderation. Riel spent several months writing a comprehensive petition with clauses concerning land rights and self-government, and at the same time was trying to press his own claims, as 240 acres (97 hectares) were owing to him in Manitoba. He also hoped to acquire an indemnity for himself, for the past services he had offered Canada, and for other injustices he had to endure. The requests of the Métis were denied. Early in 1885 the Métis learned only that they were to be enumerated, and that the greatest generosity they could expect was a chance to purchase what they believed they already owned. While D.N. Sprague views these measures as deliberate provocation, Flanagan sees these as conciliatory actions, under which the Métis were treated more liberally than the law strictly required.

Frustrated by the lack of federal action, the Métis began to talk of the use of force, and support from other settlers, and the clergy fell away. They seized arms and ammunition, took some prisoners, and on 19 March, elected a provisional government. Several days later, Frederick Middleton, commanding the Canadian military, received orders to put the militia onto alert. The first confrontation broke out at Duck Lake when the Métis encountered a government force commanded by the NWMP. Upon news of this, more than 5,000 men were mobilized, constituting the largest such preparation for war ever to take place on Canadian soil in the post-Confederation era. In early April, news of the deaths at Frog Lake, and of the captivity of two white women, aroused horror in Eastern Canada. There were several confrontations, but the decisive battle took place at Batoche on 9–12 May, and the Métis resistance was over. Riel surrendered on 15 May. The last task of the Field Force was to pursue the group of Cree who had taken the women captive, but they had to give up this task, finding it to be an impossibility over difficult and unknown terrain. The captives were all eventually freed unharmed by the Cree. Riel was tried for high treason, which under the medieval English statute of 1352 carried a mandatory death penalty. He was found guilty, and was hanged in Regina in November. Also hanged later that month were eight Cree found guilty of offences, particularly of the deaths at Frog Lake.

The Many Faces of Louis Riel

Louis Riel has been cast in a great number of contrasting lights, during his own time and after. He has been depicted as a selfish man, who led the Métis in 1885 into another unnecessary fight that served only to accelerate the dispersion and disintegration of his people. He has been dismissed as a religious fanatic. He has been celebrated as an advocate of justice for the Métis, as an astute defender of Aboriginal people, and by others as a symbol of the rights of the francophone Catholics in Canada. He has been described as an integrationist, who wanted his people to have a share in the economy and society of the new order. Riel has also been depicted as a pioneer of Western protest movements directed against the political and economic power of central Canada. He has been described as undoubtedly insane by some who have consulted evidence found in the records of his asylum years, and his diaries, while others see Riel as a man at odds with an insane and irresponsible government. According to Sprague, everything was done during Riel's lifetime (and since) to affix the blame upon Riel alone, in order to divert public attention from Métis grievances, and so that Macdonald could absolve himself and his government for the years of neglect. There has been much controversy over the issue of whether he received a fair trial. Everything possible was done to ensure Riel's conviction, according to some scholars, while others have argued that he was justly found guilty, and that there was nothing improper about the trial.

Louis Riel continues to inflame opinion in Canada. As this book was being written his name was appearing in newspaper headlines across the country. The federal government recently proclaimed in a 'Statement of Reconciliation with Aboriginal Peoples of Canada' that it wanted to acknowledge Riel's contribution to Canadian history. He may be declared a Father of Confederation, or he may be granted a posthumous pardon, or both. These announcements have met with a storm of protest, as well as declarations of support. It is of grave concern to some critics that Canada could appear to be honouring a rebel who declared that he and his followers constituted a state outside the Dominion. Separatists in Quebec could then take this as an example of a legitimate, honourable measure. There are many others who feel Riel should be recognized and honoured, for, as he himself said at his 1885 trial, 'through the grace of God I am the founder of Manitoba.'

Some of the most recent studies of the Métis west of Manitoba have shifted focus away from Riel and taken a broader approach, examining the social and economic histories of Métis communities, demonstrating that Métis history did not end in 1885, and that there has been an undue emphasis upon Riel, the Métis of Red River, and of the South Saskatchewan settlements. Historian Diane Payment has shown that, while the events of 1885 at Batoche were

devastating, the community persisted well into the twentieth century, although it increasingly became a social and
economic liability in the West to be of mixed ancestry. Payment's work has also shown that the Métis were of several
classes, and that the more affluent tended not to have been
among Riel's supporters.

While the Métis persisted, and have emerged again in
recent years to show great political energy and skill, they
had to contend with a century-long era when the great
majority were landless and impoverished, and lived on the
fringes of Indian reserves and white settlements, and on
road allowances. They were dealt with very differently from
those who were defined as Indians. Although it was recognized that the Métis had Aboriginal rights, these were
extinguished through unilateral government action and on
an individual basis, not through negotiation and treaty and
on a collective basis. The Métis of the Northwest were the
beneficiaries of certificates called 'scrip.' Métis children
born before a specified date and heads of households
could chose land scrip which entitled their possessors to a
specified number of acres of Dominion land, or money
scrip, which could be applied to the purchase of or down-
payment on land. The history of the allotment and distribution of scrip is long and complex, but the outcome was
overwhelmingly not beneficial to the Métis, as most of the
scrip quickly passed into the hands of speculators, and
the Métis were left landless. Their numbers were also
augmented in these years through concerted government
efforts to promote the withdrawal from treaty of Métis who
had taken treaty and adopted the status of Indians.

Indian Reserve Residents and 1885

The great majority of Aboriginal people took no part in the
confrontation of 1885. Treaty obligations had made First
Nations full partners in the establishment of the new legal
order. First Nations had not taken part in the earlier Métis

armed resistance in Manitoba either, even though they had no treaties at that time to honour. First Nations leaders did not wish to become involved, and counselled their people to this effect. Many sent pledges to Ottawa declaring that they did not intend to engage in hostilities. There were widespread fears among non-Aboriginal people, however, both local and distant, that a general uprising was imminent. Fed on a steady diet through the press of often sensationalized accounts of the uprisings of indigenous people in other parts of the British Empire, and of the brutality of American Indian warfare, non-Aboriginal people were prepared to see concerted and fearful developments. The so-called Siege of Fort Battleford is a case in point. As historian Walter Hildebrandt has argued, the residents of the town and district of Battleford, where there was a NWMP post, were convinced that the Cree were preparing to destroy the settlement and its inhabitants, and they barricaded themselves in the fort. A near-hysterical situation prevailed within the walls of the post as the intelligence gathered from the world beyond seemed to confirm that a concerted uprising was in the making. They saw themselves as, and in the press they were likened to, the besieged white residents of Lucknow, in the India rebellion of twenty-eight years earlier. Whatever looting took place that spring would never have happened but for the fact that the new settlers fled in panic, abandoning their homes. The Aboriginal people of the Battleford district were in such desperation for food in the spring of 1885 that some even approached the 'besieged' fort to ask for supplies. The terrified refugees were 'relieved' by the arrival of a column of the Field Force late in April, under the command of Colonel Otter, just as the besieged of Lucknow were finally relieved. No siege ever took place; this existed only in the minds of the people behind the barricades, yet the idea prevailed and was sustained in histories that were grounded in the reminiscences of those within the stockade. This was perhaps to justify the unauthorized and unprovoked military attack

Otter (unsuccessfully) launched on the Cree chief Pound-maker and his camp. As Hildebrandt has also shown, the visual art produced during the confrontation of 1885, which has been widely and uncritically used since, conveyed ideas of Indian participation and savagery, further providing justification for the attack on Poundmaker.

Also feeding fears of a general uprising were the fabricated accounts of the Cree's mistreatment of two white women widowed at Frog Lake, Theresa Delaney and Theresa Gowanlock, who were among the greatest celebrities of 1885. To many readers of the sensationalized press accounts, the whole campaign must have appeared as a heroic crusade to save the white women. It was first rumoured that they had been killed, then that they were being fearfully abused, repeatedly being made to suffer a 'fate worse than death.' Hysteria over the fate of the white women helped to cultivate hatred against the 'enemy,' bolstering military resolve and national accord. As in other parts of the British Empire where there were serious challenges to colonial authority, frenzy over the safety of white women dramatically increased, and invented stories of assault and humiliation took hold of the imagination. The women safely emerged from their admittedly unpleasant and unhappy ordeal, however, to state that they had been well treated under the circumstances; that they had not been subjected to any indignities; that they had coped reasonably well, and had enjoyed very attentive care and assistance from certain Métis families. In her first public statements, one of the women placed much of the blame for events at Frog Lake upon the shoulders of distant and indifferent government administrators. Yet quite the opposite version of their story became embedded in the public imagination, and was confirmed in the widows' book, *Two Months in the Camp of Big Bear*, published in November 1885. This presented a classic Indian captivity tale of barbaric savages and helpless white women, of a benevolent government, and sinister, plotting, subversive Métis.

Excerpts from the book were printed in Ontario papers the same month as the hangings of Riel and eight Aboriginal men, and the story served to justify these and subsequent repressive measures.

Through the press attention given to the imagined experiences of Mrs Delaney and Mrs Gowanlock in 1885, Aboriginal males were projected as a potential menace to the honour of white women, as well as being portrayed as the most savage of warriors. Aboriginal women were also presented during and after 1885 in a new, utterly fabricated, and powerfully negative light, as actively participating in some of the most violent and brutal acts against the white soldiers. These tales that were widely circulated drew upon a stockpile of horror stories from the British imperial experience. The two white women captives, by contrast, came to symbolize all that non-Aboriginal Canada held dear – the moral and cultural heart and hope of the future of the new nation. All of these representations helped cement determination that boundaries between Aboriginal and non-Aboriginal would have to be clarified and rigidly maintained.

As John Tobias has written, the idea of a general uprising was used and manipulated by government officials, most notably Edgar Dewdney, to 'declare war on the bands and leaders who had led the Cree movement for treaty revision.' Dewdney privately admitted that events at Frog Lake and the 'seige' of Battleford were the acts of a desperate and starving people, but publicly proclaimed that the Cree were part of the Métis uprising. With Big Bear and Poundmaker in custody, Dewdney could use the courts to destroy Cree leadership, a plan of his that pre-dated the events of 1885. Both were charged with treason-felony and sent to prison, despite the fact the Dewdney was well aware that neither man had engaged in an act of rebellion. After their release both soon died from tuberculosis contracted while inside. The trials of the more than fifty Indians accused of various degrees of involvement in the confrontation of

1885 have been described in a recent history as a travesty. Very few had legal counsel, and they understood little or nothing of what was said or argued as it was all in English and a translator was used sparingly. Sentences were severe and in contradiction of standard practice. For example, one man received six years for stealing a horse, another fourteen years for arson.

A mass execution of eight Aboriginal men was held at Battleford NWMP post in November 1885. The intention was to have a public spectacle that would convey a clear message as to who was now completely in control. The assistant commissioner, Hayter Reed, wrote, 'I am desirous of having the Indians witness it – No sound threshing having been given them I think a sight of this sort would cause them to meditate for many a day.' Such a spectacle was not accepted Canadian, or international, practice at the time, and there were many in Canada who found it deplorable. In the editorials of several Eastern newspapers, the execution of eight people was condemned as unworthy of a civilized nation, and as carrying bloodthirstiness too far.

An Administered People: The Aftermath of 1885

Historians who have examined various aspects of the emerging Canadian West in the 1880s, including the press, the NWMP, and Department of Indian Affairs, have detected a significant shift in Euro-Canadian attitudes towards Aboriginal people after 1885. If there was a shred of tolerance before, or the possibility of working towards a progressive partnership, it was shattered in 1885, as thereafter Aboriginal people were viewed as a threat to the property and safety of the white settlers.

In the immediate aftermath of 1885, there was spirited debate about the administration of Indian affairs in the Northwest, with charges of gross injustice and incompetence levelled, but the government did little to seriously and thoroughly investigate past approaches, and admitted to no mistakes. Instead, efforts to create a sterling public image were stepped up, as were initiatives aimed at rigidly controlling and monitoring the lives of the people who lived on Indian reserves, and at destroying their social and cultural integrity, and forms of leadership. Hayter Reed, in consultation with Edgar Dewdney, was a major architect of what they termed the 'assault upon the tribal system.' Reed was an Indian agent at Battleford, then rose through the ranks, becoming assistant commissioner in 1884, commissioner in 1888, and deputy superintendent general in 1893. He believed that there never had been any grounds for complaint among Indians; any dissent and dissatisfaction was due to nefarious 'outside agitators,' which usually meant the Métis.

The major goals of government policy in the aftermath of 1885 were to wage war upon what was called the 'tribal' system and to rigidly supervise and monitor the movements and activities of reserve people. In a speech he gave in the 1890s, Reed described the Indians as a 'foreign element' who constituted a source of danger. They had to be broken up, disbanded, assimilated. These were by no means entirely new goals and initiatives, but after 1885 they were pursued with great vigour. Independence, and a proprietary spirit, were to be fostered in several ways. The reserves were to be subdivided into 40-acre (16-hectare) plots and certificates of ownership, even though they did not signify outright ownership, were to be issued. There was to be 'family farming' with a male head of household farmer, and the wife as the individual homemaker. A policy of undermining the traditional system of leadership was to be pursued. To enhance the ability of government officials to supervise the Indians, the number of NWMP in the West was greatly increased, as were the number of Indian Department employees.

The most notorious of the post-1885 measures was the pass system, first initiated on a large scale during the crisis of 1885. Those who wished to leave their reserves were required to obtain passes from the agent or farm instructor declaring the purpose of their absence, the length of absence, and whether or not they had permission to carry arms. The pass system was never a law; it was never codified in the Indian Act, and it can only be described as a 'policy.' From the time of the earliest discussions about such a system, there was recognition among officials that it ran directly counter to the treaties and had no validity in law. Official rationales advanced for maintaining the system after 1885 were that Indians had to be kept separate from the rest of society for their own good, as contact tended to be injurious to them. Reserve farmers could be made to remain with their crops at critical times. It was also retained after 1885 to prevent future 'rebellious' movements, and in response to the non-Aboriginal public which demanded that the spheres be kept separate. There were even calls for 'Indian Removal' to the northerly regions.

The pass system, its pervasiveness and effectiveness, has generated considerable debate among historians. The larger issue is: to what extent were these admittedly coercive policies successful in achieving the goals for which they were devised? The argument that Aboriginal people were active agents, refusing to be victimized, is stressed by those who contend that the pass system was ineffective. F. Laurie Barron and J.R. Miller have contended that the pass system was a nullity, that the police were reluctant to enforce it, that department officials did not have the time to do so, and that reserve residents, as 'active agents,' ignored the regulation, simply going where they wanted to or cynically obtaining passes. My own research suggests a different interpretation, which is that, just as in other colonial settings, such as South Africa and Kenya, the pass system operated to separate white people from indigenous people, and to carefully monitor how, where, and when contact would be permitted to take place. The pass system was not enforced with the same rigour at all times and in all locations of the West; indeed, it was a preserve of the southern 'settlement belt.' There is evidence that it was still in use into the 1940s, and that the non-Aboriginal public demanded it. The police admittedly found it difficult at times to enforce, and a solution that they advanced was to abolish it altogether, providing no opportunity for people to leave their reserves. Oral and written testimony from reserve residents indicates that it was both enforced and resented as a result. As Dan Kennedy wrote, 'In the early days of reservation life, the Indians were plagued with all kinds of restrictions, imposed on them by the guardian government. ... We also had to get passes from the Indian Agent to go anywhere on social visits or business trips. The Indian reserve was a veritable concentration camp.' There are stories that celebrated the ability of individuals to circumvent this and other policies, and regulations, but these should not be mistakenly understood to represent the broader situation. The pass system was an effective mechanism for keeping people on their reserves. Along with other informal and formal policies, it limited the mobility and economic opportunities of reserve residents. Employment and marketing opportunities were limited. Also in clear violation of treaty rights, the 1893 Game Ordinance of the Territorial government combined with an amendment to the Indian Act to restrict Indian game hunting, which further limited people's reasons to move off-reserve and dramatically reduced the resources available to them.

Another law introduced in 1885 was an amendment to the Indian Act which banned the potlatch, a central ceremony of the coastal people of British Columbia, and thereafter a series of amendments were made that were designed to eliminate religious expression and ceremonies such as the Sun Dance, and giveaway ceremonies of the prairies. The rationale, according to Katherine Pettipas, was the recognition that there was a direct connection between ceremonial life and the political, economic, social, and cultural integrity of indigenous societies. As with the pass system, there are debates about the effectiveness of these laws. There was prolonged and determined resistance to them, but government efforts were also sustained and pervasive. Pettipas documents the many mechanisms aside from arrest, conviction, and incarceration that were used to discourage ceremonial practice, including the pass system, police patrols, restricted access to material goods for ceremonies, the destruction of sacred offerings and lodges, and the enforced dispersal of groups.

Formal education was also used to erode indigenous religious ceremonies and foster assimilation. Until the 1950s on the prairies, education for the vast majority of Indian children was segregated. They attended schools established under the auspices of the federal Indian Department, with the active cooperation of Christian denominations, while for all other children schooling was a provincial responsibility. Industrial schools, established in Western Canada in the early 1880s, were the jewel of the government's program of assimilation. Students spent half the day on academic pursuits, and the other half on learning skills and trades. Boys learned carpentry, farming, blacksmithing, and, later on, shoemaking. Girls learned such household skills as laundry, cooking, and sewing. The work of both boys and girls was essential to the maintenance of the schools. At the Red Deer Industrial School, for example, the boys cut thousands of rails for fencing, built fences, dug up stumps, and cleared away the brush. Girls made the uniforms worn by the students and cooked meals for staff and inmates. The number of industrial schools expanded rapidly in the 1880s and 1890s, but enthusiasm for them waned by the last years of the century because of a combination of disappointing results and escalating costs. They were expensive to run, even though the students did much of the work and costs were kept to a minimum. Wages were kept low for the teachers, who received about half the average salary of other teachers on the prairies. It was difficult to get competent teachers under these circumstances.

Recruiting students was difficult. Parents were not enthusiastic about sending their children because, in the earliest years of the program, they were not permitted any holidays at all. As well, the use of corporal punishment was a concern. There was also a high rate of desertion from the institutions, with parents sometimes demanding that their children be permitted to return home. Amendments to the Indian Act in 1894 allowed the department to make regulations regarding attendance at schools. Students at residential and industrial schools were also lost through the high death rate owing to diseases such as tuberculosis. In 1895, for example, 65 per cent of the children at Crowstand School in the Swan River agency were afflicted with tuberculosis. Nearly one-third of the Red Deer Industrial School students of the early 1890s died at the school, immediately upon leaving it, or within one decade of leaving it. The schools had well-populated cemeteries that in many cases remain today the only remnant of these institutions. The government began to abandon the concept of industrial schools by the early twentieth century, although residential schools remained in operation well into the twentieth century.

There was also an alarming death rate on the reserves. The more northerly people, who had not been dependent on the buffalo and who continued to hunt and fish, did not suffer health problems to the same extent as those to the south. From the mid-1880s, reserve groups experienced a significant population loss that continued well into the twentieth century. Maureen Lux writes, 'Malnutrition, overcrowding, exposure, poor sanitation, and oppressive government policies reduced populations on most reserves by 30% to 50%. Very often infant and child mortality outstripped the birth rate.' The diseases included tuberculosis, whooping cough, measles, influenza, and pneumonia. A form of scurvy resulting from the exclusive use of salt pork caused a great number of deaths in the early reserve years. Exacerbating all of this were living conditions that were as poor as, or poorer than, those in the worst urban slums of the nineteenth century. People lived in low, one-storey, one-room log shacks, with stoves and chimneys made of clay for heat and ventilation. The walls were plastered with mud and hay, and they had no flooring. The roofs were constructed with logs or poles over which rows of straw or grass were laid.

Indian Department officials responded to these conditions and to their critics by stepping up efforts to polish a sterling public image. Maureen Lux has found, for example, that there was deliberate manipulation of the published statistical record to reduce the very high death rates for 1895. The reports of Indian agents were also edited for publication, as they were to divulge only that 'which it was desired the public should believe.' Blame for faltering reserve economies, and for poor living conditions, was assigned to Aboriginal people themselves, who would not take steps to improve their situation. The men refused to farm. They had no habits of thrift and perseverance. Reserve women were cast as poor housekeepers; the high infant mortality rate and the tuberculosis epidemic were all attributed to their supposedly deficient housekeeping, parenting, and nursing skills.

Not all Indian Affairs officials shared and promoted these views. Many of the 'men on the spot,' the agents and farm instructors, were sympathetic to the people they worked with, and were just as frustrated with the distant policymakers. A number of Indian agents, especially those in the first generation of reserve employees, worked very hard to assist in establishing reserve agriculture, and they were also important vocal advocates for the interests of Indians. They helped to push for some of the assistance that allowed reserve agriculture to briefly progress in the late 1880s.

In the face of all of the obstacles, restrictions, and problems reserve residents had to contend with, they took what action they could to build economies, and to diversify their skills. Both men and women clearly wished to acquire the skills and equipment essential to rural life in the West. At no time did they adopt a policy of passive submission, lack of interest, or apathy. Their spokespersons continued to protest and petition at every opportunity, even though the department took steps to limit these opportunities. They also resisted intrusions upon their cultural integrity, and continued to some extent to practise their sacred ceremonies, finding ways to circumvent regulations.

Pressures of Competition and 'Peasant' Farming

By the late 1880s reserve farmers in some localities began to make significant advances, having produce that they wished to sell: predominantly cattle, grain, and hay. They acquired some of the up-to-date machinery needed to enhance their enterprises, such as mowers and rakes, reapers and self-binders, purchased through pooled annuities or other earnings. Such machinery allowed farmers to increase their acreage under cultivation, and some farmers sold hay on contract. At this time, however, non-Aboriginal farmers began to complain loudly about 'unfair' competition from Aboriginal people, arguing they they should not be allowed to compete with other settlers in the sale of products such as hay, grain, and potatoes. Concern was also expressed that, if reserve residents were allowed to become successful stock raisers, those who supplied beef on contract for rationing would be deprived of their livelihood. In 1888 the editor of the Battleford *Saskatchewan Herald* denounced any plan to 'set the Indians up as cattle breeders, encouraging them to supply the beef that is now put in by white contractors.'

In 1889, Hayter Reed responded to the concerns of non-Aboriginal residents and announced a new system of farming. Reserve farmers were to reduce their acreage to a single acre, and their herds to a cow or two, emulating peasants of other countries. They were to use rudimentary implements alone: to broadcast seed by hand, harvest with scythes, bind by hand with straw, thresh with flails, and

grind their grain with hand mills. They were to manufacture for themselves implements such as harrows, hay
forks, carts, and yokes. Publicly the policy was justified as
an approach that would render reserve residents self-
·supporting, implanting self-reliance and individualism.
Reed argued that labour-saving machinery might be
necessary for other farmers, but Indians had to first experience farming with crude and simple implements. Other-
wise they would be defying immutable laws of evolution,
and would be making an 'unnatural leap.' Clearly, however, there were other reasons for the peasant farming for-
mula, reasons that were understood and appreciated by
non-Aboriginal farmers. In 1887 the *Saskatchewan Herald*
applauded the policy for the Aboriginal farmer: 'Thrown
thus on himself and left to work his farm without the aid of
expensive machinery he will content himself with raising
just what he needs himself, and thus while meeting the
Government's intention of becoming self-sustaining, they
at the same time would come into competition with the
white settler only to the extent of their own labour, and
thus remove all grounds for the complaint being made in
some quarters against Government aided Indians entering
into competition with white settlers.'

Aboriginal farmers, Indian agents, farm instructors, and
inspectors of agencies all protested this policy, but these
protests were ignored, and it was implemented on Plains
reserves until just after the change of government in 1896.
Officials in the field were dismayed by a policy that robbed
the reserve farmers of any potential source of revenue.
The farmers themselves were profoundly discouraged by
the new rules. Many aspects of the program were simply
unworkable, even laughable. At headquarters in Ottawa, it
proved impossible to acquire some of the old-fashioned
implements such as hand mills. Hayter Reed, however, was
not moved by the objections and complaints, and refused
to give in to the 'whims of farmers and Indians.' By the
mid-1890s, per-capita acreage under cultivation had fallen

to about half of the 1889 level, and many acres once under cultivation on reserves were idle. The government had acted not to promote the agriculture of the indigenous population but to provide an optimum environment for the immigrant settler. Aboriginal people protested these policies that adversely affected them. They raised objections to government officials, petitioned the House of Commons, sent letters to newspapers, and visited Ottawa.

These policies and restrictions upon economic independence weighed heavily upon people, and they were resented. Cree authors Joe Dion and Edward Ahenakew wrote about how regulations crippled initiative, and created a discouraged people. Dion believed that, because of the permit system and other regulations, the cattle industry on his reserve died, and many discontinued farming entirely. He wrote that it was 'small wonder that the best men in our ranks eventually got discouraged and simply gave up trying because even the most humble wage earner will resist a domineering employer when his direct supervision gets to be a hindrance rather than an asset.' Aboriginal people had agency, of course, but so did the government and its agents, and the latter enjoyed considerably more power, strength, and influence. Government authorities proved extremely resourceful, industrious, and flexible in devising new strategies that could further limit avenues of protest. By the 1890s department officials were instructed not to convene or be present at meetings with reserve farmers, and agents and instructors risked dismissal if they refused to comply with the peasant farming policy. The policy was not applied to all reserves in Western Canada. It appears to have been most heavily imposed on the more southerly reserves, where agriculture had shown some signs of progress.

North of the Tree Line

A widely accepted generalization concerning the people of

the boreal forest in the post-treaty era is that they continued to experience the 'traditional' life of hunting, trapping, and fishing, much as they had before, because there were not the same pressures of intensive settlement, and that the full weight of Indian Act restrictions and other regulations did not fall upon them until well into the twentieth century, if at all. Arthur J. Ray has written that the experience of the people of the boreal forest is fundamentally different from that of other more southerly Aboriginal groups, as they were not pushed off the land for agricultural settlement, their languages continue to flourish, and such forces as missionaries and government agents had little impact on them before the early part of the twentieth century. Yet, in his study of Indians and the fur trade Ray argued that the people of the forested regions became dependent upon the posts to a much greater degree than did the people of the Plains. The fur trade did not stop with the transfer of 1870 for the people of the boreal forest and they were very much affected by outside developments, such as fluctuations in the demand for furs. As the twentieth century dawned, the HBC faced formidable rivals for furs, such as Révillon Frères of Paris, who established a network of posts that covered most of the subarctic. This rush for furs had some very adverse long-term effects on Aboriginal economies.

In his study of northern Manitoba in the post-1870 era, Frank Tough shows that by the time of treaty talks of the 1870s, and well before, there was no 'traditional' life, as people had been involved in the industry of the fur trade for 200 years. In the Treaty Five region of central–northern Manitoba, there was a rapidly changing economy after 1870 that was quite different from the fur-trade regime – steamboat harbours, fish stations, and sawmills soon dotted the landscape. In the early reserve-transition era, Aboriginal people became involved in wage labour, lumbering, and commercial fishing, and they also gardened and kept cattle. They played a vital role in the 'opening-up' of northern

Manitoba. However, they did not have control over the regional economy. In fact, in the unceded territory to the north of the boundaries of Treaty Five, Aboriginal people were, according to Tough, 'trapped in a traditional economy and suffered serious periodic shortages, low prices for furs, and diminished wage employment.'

Focusing on the Fort Chipewyan region in northwestern Alberta from 1870, Patricia A. McCormack has documented the process through which the Canadian and later provincial governments expanded into this region, creating a powerful new administrative framework that replaced the fur trade and restricted Aboriginal access to the land and its resources. This process took many decades but began with the Canadian government's 1870 purchase of the territory from the HBC, and with Treaty Eight (1899). McCormack also documents the many strategies that Northerners adopted to challenge and circumvent government agents and regulations. Not all groups in the north, however, were visited by treaty commissioners. The Lubicon Cree of northern Alberta, for example, did not meet with any Indian Affairs officials until 1939. The issue of the recognition of their rights and claims to their territory remained unsettled throughout the twentieth century, at a time when there were devastating changes to their economy because of resource development.

Paths Diverge

The Wilfrid Laurier Liberals were fortunate to win the election of June 1896 just at the dawn of this new age of prosperity for Canada, and Western Canada in particular. Conditions favourable to the national policy of industrialization, east–west railway traffic, and Western settlement at last came into being. The end of a drought cycle and improvements in dry-land farming techniques ushered in a wheat boom. The Canadian prairies became the site of the last great land rush in North American history, and the

Aboriginal inhabitants became a small minority of the population. It was clear by the later 1890s that the Aboriginal
residents would not share in the new prosperity. As land
values in the West rose dramatically, there appeared to be
even less inclination to share the bounty than was evident
in the much leaner years of the previous decades. The new
federal administrators were not at all interested in foster-
ing stable reserve economies. The Liberals slashed the
budget for Indian Affairs, dismissing many employees and
lowering the salaries of those who remained. The new
administration became preoccupied with encouraging
reserve land 'surrender,' and they succeeded in diminish-
ing the size of many reserves in the West, particularly those
with agricultural potential.

From the mid-1890s the disparities between the way
most non-Aboriginal and Aboriginal Westerners lived and
worked increased dramatically. The experience of living on
federally administered reserves was quite distinct from the
experiences of all other people who came to dwell in Western Canada. People were almost completely physically or
spatially separated; even towns became less frequently
zones of interaction, and Aboriginal activities off-reserve
were monitored by police and government agents. There
were fewer opportunities for 'integration.' This was
reflected in the new goals for the education of Indians –
they were to be taught applied skills that could be used in
their everyday lives, and be equipped, not to take jobs off-
reserve, but to return to their own communities. People
were also separated through the now deeply embedded stereotypes, misconceptions, and suspicions that each side
had of the other. Non-Aboriginal Westerners had very little
actual knowledge of the First Peoples, but they were well
equipped with a set of beliefs and 'folk wisdom' that they
shared and expressed among themselves. One of the most
persistent ideas is that Aboriginal people are themselves to
blame for whatever misfortunes they may have experienced, as they were given every opportunity, were even

'coddled' by government, but were simply unable to change and adapt, as they clung to their 'traditional' ways, and this made them entirely unsuited to 'modern' pursuits – farming, for example. These ideas have, in various guises, also appeared in academic studies.

The experiences of the Cree Almighty Voice, or Kitchimanito-waya, has been viewed by a number of historians as symbolic of the end of an era in Western Canada. The story has tremendous dramatic content, a fact not lost to the motion picture industry. A feature film about this incident, *Alien Thunder*, starring Donald Sutherland, Gordon Tootoosis, and Chief Dan George, was made in the 1970s just outside Saskatoon, although it was a box-office failure. In 1895 Almighty Voice, a young man of about twenty-two, was arrested for having killed a steer. He escaped from the tiny prison at Duck Lake (which can be visited today), and became the object of an intensive manhunt after he shot and killed a Mountie who had attempted to arrest him. But Almighty Voice eluded all efforts to catch him. It was not until the spring of 1897 that he and two companions were located in the Minichinas Hills, just a few miles from Batoche. They seriously wounded two Mounted Police officers who located them, and were soon surrounded by a force of twenty-four Mounties, a nine-pound gun, and an artillery team. While hundreds of local residents looked on, this force bombarded the grove where the three Cree had dug themselves in, while Almighty Voice's mother sat on a a hill nearby, singing her son's war song. When the police rushed the bluff following the bombardment, they found the bodies of Almighty Voice, his brother-in-law, and his cousin.

The story of Almighty Voice has often been depicted in an exceedingly romantic light. His desperate and murderous flight is seen as the 'last stand' of a man who could not cope and adjust to new conditions, who could not understand and would not accept that the buffalo, the freedom of riding anywhere on the Plains, and the excitement of warfare were all in the past. The romantic and the nostalgic Indian who would not adjust and accept his fate, and therefore turned his back on the new world of opportunities, has proven much more palatable to non-Aboriginal people than one who had good reason to resist and protest policies that deliberately denied these opportunities. Almighty Voice's troubles began when he was arrested for having killed a steer on the One Arrow Reserve. He had contended that he had committed no crime, and that the steer in fact belonged to his father, and not the government. It was eventually admitted by authorities that the original charge was mistaken. Almighty Voice's protest could be seen, not in the futile 'last stand' light, but as an effort to draw attention to the policies and practices such as the permit system that restricted the basic freedoms of people defined as Indians, denying them even the right to slaughter their own beef cattle.

The image of a large contingent of Mounties, surrounded by 'citizen' onlookers, bombarding a grove of trees and killing three young Cree men, is a disturbing one to those who cherish the idea of Canada's kinder and gentler history. To reach this conclusion, only highly selective examples can be used. Over 100 years later Aboriginal people are still embroiled in struggles across Canada to regain and retain their rights to land and resources. An understanding of the formative years of Aboriginal and non-Aboriginal relations to the end of the late nineteenth century is critical to an appreciation of how we have arrived here and how change may be initiated.

Bibliography

General Works/ Overviews

Dickason, Olive P. *Canada's First Nations: A History of Founding Peoples from Earliest Times*, 2d ed. Toronto: McClelland & Stewart, 1996.

Friesen, Gerald. *The Canadian Prairies: A History.* Toronto: University of Toronto Press, 1984.

Kehoe, Alice B. *North American Indians: A Comprehensive Account*, 2d ed., Toronto: Prentice-Hall, 1992.

Miller, J.R. *Skyscrapers Hide the Heavens: A History of Indian–White Relations in Canada.* Toronto: University of Toronto Press, 1989.

Ray, A.J. *'I Have Lived Here Since the World Began': An Illustrated History of Canada's Native People.* Toronto: Lester Publishing, 1996.

Trigger, Bruce G., and Wilcomb E. Washburn, eds. *The Cambridge History of the Native Peoples of the Americas*, 2 vols. New York: Cambridge University Press, 1996.

Introduction

Brownlie, Robin, and Mary-Ellen Kelm. 'Desperately Seeking Absolution: Native Agency as Colonialist Alibi?' *Canadian Historical Review* 75/4 (1994): 543–56.

Chartrand, Paul. '"Terms of Division": Problems of "Outside

Naming" for Aboriginal People in Canada.' *Journal of Indigenous Studies* 2/2 (1991): 1–22.

Trigger, Bruce G. 'Early Native North American Responses to European Contact: Romantic versus Rationalistic Interpretations.' *Journal of American History* 77 (1991): 1195–1215.

Welsh, Christine. 'Voices of the Grandmothers: Reclaiming a Metis Heritage.' *Canadian Literature* 131 (1991): 15–24.

Chapter 1   Homeland

Bryan, Liz. *The Buffalo People: Prehistoric Archaeology on the Canadian Plains.* Edmonton: University of Alberta Press, 1991.

Cleland, Charles E. *Rites of Conquest: The History and Culture of Michigan's Native Americans.* Ann Arbor: University of Michigan Press, 1992.

Cowie, Isaac. *The Company of Adventurers: A Narrative of Seven Years in the Service of the Hudson's Bay Company during 1867–1874 on the Great Buffalo Plains.* Toronto: William Briggs, 1913.

Deloria, Vine, Jr. *Red Earth, White Lies: Native Americans and the Myth of Scientific Fact.* New York: Scribner's, 1995.

Duke, Philip. *Points in Time: Structure and Event in Late Northern Plains Hunting Society.* Niwot: University of Colorado Press, 1991.

Flynn, Catherine, and E. Leigh Syms. 'Manitoba's First Farmers.' *Manitoba History* (Spring 1996): 4–11.

Geist, Valerius. *Buffalo Nation: History and Legend of the North American Bison.* Saskatoon: Fifth House, 1996.

Malainey, Mary E., and Barbara L. Sherriff. 'Adjusting Our Perceptions: Historical and Archaeological Evidence of Winter on the Plains of Western Canada.' *Plains Anthropologist* 41/158 (1996): 333–57.

Spector, Janet D. *What This Awl Means: Feminist Archaeology at a Wapeton Dakota Village.* St Paul: Minnesota Historical Society Press, 1993.

Vansina, Jan. *Oral Tradition as History.* Madison: University of Wisconsin Press, 1985.

Chapter 2   Worlds Intersect

Crosby, Alfred W. *The Columbian Exchange: Biological and Cultural Consequences of 1492*. Westport, CT: Greenwood 1972.

Dion, Joe. *My Tribe the Crees*. Calgary: Glenbow-Alberta Institute, 1979.

Dobyns, Henry F. *'Their Number Become Thinned': Native American Population Dynamics in Eastern North America*. Knoxville: University of Tennessee Press, 1983.

Kennedy, Dan. *Recollections of an Assiniboine Chief*. Toronto: McClelland & Stewart, 1972.

MacLaren, Ian. '"I Came to Rite Thare Portraits": Paul Kane's Journal of His Western Travels, 1846–1848.' *The American Art Journal* 21/2 (1989): 7–19.

MacLeod, D. Peter. 'The Amerindian Discovery of Europe: Accounts of First Contact in Anishinabeg Oral Tradition.' In *The Invention of Canada: Readings in Pre-Confederation History*, ed. Chad Gaffield, 53–9. Toronto: Copp Clark Longman, 1994.

Morton, W.L. *Manitoba: A History*. Toronto: University of Toronto Press, 1957.

Rollason, Heather Ann. 'Staying under the Influence: The Impact of Samuel Hearne's Journal on the Scholarly Literature about Chipewyan Women.' Unpublished MA thesis, Trent University, 1994.

Sundstrom, Linea. 'Smallpox Used Them Up: References to Epidemic Disease in Northern Plains Winter Counts, 1714–1920.' *Ethnohistory* 44/2 (Spring 1997): 305–29.

Warkentin, Germaine, ed. *Canadian Exploration Literature: An Anthology*. Toronto: Oxford University Press, 1993.

White, Richard. *The Middle Ground: Indians, Empires, and Republics in the Great Lakes Region, 1650–1815*. New York: Cambridge University Press, 1991.

Chapter 3   Fur-Trade Interaction

Bourgeault, Ron. 'Race, Class and Gender: Colonial Domination of Indian Women.' In *Race, Class, Gender: Bonds and Barriers*,

ed. Jesse Vorst et al., 87–115. Winnipeg: Society for Socialist
Studies, 1989.

Brown, Jennifer. 'Fur Trade History as Text and Drama.' In *The
Uncovered Past: Roots of Northern Alberta Societies*, ed. Patricia A.
McCormack and R. Geoffrey Ironsides, 81–8. Edmonton:
Canadian Circumpolar Institute, 1993.

– *Strangers in Blood: Fur Trade Company Families in Indian Country.*
Vancouver: University of British Columbia Press, 1980.

Finlay, J.L., and D.N. Sprague. *The Structure of Canadian History*,
5th ed. Scarborough: Prentice-Hall Allyn/Bacon, 1997.

Kehoe, Alice. 'Ethnicity at a Pedlar's Post in Saskatchewan.' *Western Canadian Journal of Anthropology* 6/1 (1976): 52–60.

Morantz, Toby. 'Old Texts, Old Questions: Another Look at the
Issue of Continuity and the Early Fur-Trade Period.' *Canadian
Historical Review* 73 (1992): 166–93.

Payne, Michael. 'Summary Report: Fur Trade and Native History
Workshop.' *Rupert's Land Research Centre Newsletter* 7/1 (1991):
7–21.

Peers, Laura. *The Ojibway of Western Canada: 1780–1870.* Winnipeg: University of Manitoba Press, 1994.

Ray, A.J. *Indians in the Fur Trade: Their Role as Trappers, Hunters,
and Middlemen in the Lands Southwest of Hudson Bay, 1660–1870.*
Toronto: University of Toronto Press, 1974. Rpt. and new
introd., 1998.

Rogers, Mary Black. 'Varities of "Starving": Semantics and Survival in the Sub-Arctic Fur Trade, 1750–1850.' *Ethnohistory* 33
(1986): 353–83.

Russell, Dale R. *Eighteenth-Century Western Cree and Their Neighbours.* Archaeological Survey of Canada Mercury Series Paper
no. 143. Ottawa: Canadian Museum of Civilization, 1991.

Smith, Erica. 'Something More than Mere Ornament: Cloth and
Indian-European Relationships in the Eighteenth Century.'
Unpublished MA thesis, University of Winnipeg/University of
Manitoba, 1991.

Smith, James G.E. 'The Western Woods Cree: Anthropological
Myth and Historical Reality.' *American Ethnologist* 14/3 (1987):
434–48.

Van Kirk, Sylvia. *'Many Tender Ties': Women in Fur Trade Society, 1670–1870.* Winnipeg: Watson and Dwyer, 1980.

Chapter 4   Cultural Crossroads: The Red River Settlement

Bain, Eleanor. 'Speech of the Lower Red River Settlement.' In *Papers of the Eighteenth Algonquian Conference,* ed. William Cowan, 7–16. Ottawa: Carleton University Press, 1987.

Bumsted, J.M. *The Red River Rebellion.* Winnipeg: Watson and Dwyer, 1996.

Cardinal, Harold. *The Unjust Society: The Tragedy of Canada's Indians.* Edmonton: Hurtig, 1969.

Coutts, Robert. 'The Forks of the Red and Assiniboine: A Thematic History, 1734–1850.' In *The Forks of the Red and Assiniboine: A History, 1734–1900,* 1–229. Ottawa: Environment Canada, Canadian Parks Service, 1988.

Davies, Wayne K.D. 'A Welsh Missionary at Canada's Red River Settlement, 1823–38.' *National Library of Wales Journal* 27 (1991–2): 217–42.

Dick, Lyle. 'The Seven Oaks Incident and the Construction of a Historical Tradition, 1816–1970.' In *Making Western Canada: Essays on Colonization and Settlement,* ed. Catherine Cavanaugh and Jeremy Mouat, 1–30. Toronto: Garamond, 1996.

Erickson, Lesley. 'At the Cultural and Religious Crossroads: Sara Riel and the Grey Nuns in the Canadian Northwest, 1848–1883.' Unpublished MA thesis, Univesity of Calgary, 1997.

Ens, Gerhard J. *Homeland to Hinterland: The Changing Worlds of the Red River Metis in the Nineteenth Century.* Toronto: University of Toronto Press, 1996.

Grant, John Webster. *Moon of Wintertime: Missionaries and the Indians of Canada in Encounter since 1534.* Toronto: University of Toronto Press, 1984.

Pannekoek, Frits. *A Snug Little Flock: The Social Origins of the Riel Resistance, 1869–70.* Winnipeg: Watson and Dwyer, 1991.

Peterson, Jacqueline, and Jennifer S.H. Brown, eds. *The New Peoples: Being and Becoming Metis in North America.* Winnipeg: The University of Manitoba Press, 1985.

Stevenson, Winona. 'The Journals and Voices of a Church of England Native Catechist: Askenootow (Charles Pratt), 1851–1884.' In *Reading Beyond Words: Contexts for Native History*, ed. Jennifer S.H. Brown and Elizabeth Vibert, 304–29. Toronto: Broadview, 1996.

West, John. *The Substance of the Journal During a Residence at a Red River Colony*. London: L.B. Seeley and Son, 1824.

Chapter 5   Change and Continuity: The World of the Plains

Binnema, Ted. 'Old Swan, Big Man, and the Siksika Bands, 1794–1815.' *Canadian Historical Review* 77/1 (1996): 1–32.

Conaty, Gerald. 'Economic Models and Blackfoot Ideology.' *American Ethnologist* 22/2 (1995): 403–12.

Dempsey, Hugh A. *Red Crow: Warrior Chief*. Saskatoon: Western Producer Prairie Books, 1980.

Dobak, William A. 'Killing the Canadian Buffalo, 1821–1881.' *Western Historical Quarterly* 27 (Spring 1996): 33–52.

Flores, Dan. 'Bison Ecology and Bison Diplomacy: The Southern Plains from 1800 to 1850.' *Journal of American History* 78/2 (1991): 465–85.

Hildebrandt, Walter, and Brian Hubner. *The Cypress Hills: The Land and Its People*. Saskatoon: Purich, 1994.

Hungry Wolf, Beverly. *The Ways of My Grandmothers*. New York: Quill, 1982.

Kehoe, Alice. 'Blackfoot Persons.' In *Woman and Power in Native North America*, ed. Laura F. Klein and Lillian A. Ackerman, 113–25. Norman and Lincoln: University of Oklahoma Press, 1995.

Klein, Alan M. 'The Political-Economy of Gender: A Nineteenth-Century Plains Indian Case Study.' In *The Hidden Half: Studies of Plains Indian Women*, ed. Patricia Albers and Beatrice Medicine, 143–73. Washington, DC: University Press of America, 1983.

Lewis, Oscar. 'The Manly-hearted Woman among the North Peigan.' *American Anthropologist* 43: 173 -87.

McDougall, John. *In the Days of the Red River Rebellion: Life and*

Adventure in the Far West of Canada. Toronto: William Briggs, 1903.

Milloy, John S. *The Plains Cree: Trade, Diplomacy and War, 1790–1870.* Winnipeg: University of Manitoba Press, 1988.

Red Crow. 'The Life History and Adventures of Red Crow Related to the late R.N. Wilson, Dec. 1891.' In *Kainai Chieftainship: History, Evolution and Culture of the Blood Indians,* ed. S.H. Middleton, 113–64. Lethbridge: Job Printing Dept., 1953.

Roe, F.G. *The North American Buffalo: A Critical Study of the Species in Its Wild State,* 2d ed. Toronto: University of Toronto Press, 1970.

Sharp, Paul F. *Whoop-Up Country: The Canadian-American West, 1865–1885.* Norman: University of Oklahoma Press, 1955.

Smits, David D. 'The Frontier Army and the Destruction of the Buffalo: 1865–1883.' *Western Historical Quarterly* 25/3 (1994): 313–38.

White, Richard. '"Are You an Environmentalist or Do You Work for a Living?"' In *Uncommon Ground: Rethinking the Human Place in Nature,* ed W. Cronon, 171–85. New York: W.W. Norton, 1995.

Chapter 6 Canada's Colony and the Colonized

Borrows, John. 'Wampum at Niagara: The Royal Proclamation, Canadian Legal History, and Self-Government.' In *Aboriginal and Treaty Rights in Canada: Essays on Law, Equality, and Respect for Difference,* ed Michael Asch, 155–72. Vancouver: University of British Columbia Press, 1997.

Cardinal, Harold. 'Treaty Eight: The Right to Livelihood.' Unpublished LLM thesis, Harvard University Law School, 1996.

Chartrand, Paul L.A.H. *Manitoba's Metis Settlement Scheme of 1870.* Saskatoon: Native Law Centre, 1991.

Flanagan, Thomas, and Gerhard J. Ens. 'Metis Land Grants in Manitoba: A Statistical Study.' *Histoire sociale/Social History* 27/23 (1994): 65–88.

Francis, R. Douglas. *Images of the West.* Saskatoon: Western Producer Prairie Books, 1989.

Friesen, Jean. 'Magnificent Gifts: The Treaties of Canada with the Indians of the Northwest, 1869–76.' *Transactions of the Royal Society of Canada*, series 5, vol. 1 (1986): 41–51.

Hildebrandt, Walter. *Views from Fort Battleford: Constructed Visions of an Anglo-Canadian West.* Regina: Canadian Plains Research Center, 1994.

Milloy, John S. 'The Early Indian Acts: Developental Strategy and Constitutional Change.' In *As Long as the Sun Shines and Water Flows,* ed. Ian A.L. Getty and Antoine S. Lussier, 56–64. Vancouver: UBC Press, 1983.

Morris, Alexander. *The Treaties of Canada with the Indians of Manitoba and the North-West Territories.* 1880. Reprint. Toronto: Coles Publishing, 1971.

Owram, Douglas. *Promise of Eden: The Canadian Expansionist Movement and the Idea of the West, 1856–1900.* Toronto: University of Toronto Press, 1980.

Sprague, D.N. *Canada and the Metis, 1869–1885.* Waterloo: Wilfrid Laurier University Press, 1988.

Stanley, G.F.G. *The Birth of Western Canada: A History of the Riel Rebellions* 1936. Reprint. Toronto: University of Toronto Press, 1975.

Tobias, John. 'Protection, Civilization, Assimilation: An Outline History of Canada's Indian Policy.' In *As Long as the Sun Shines and Water Flows,* ed. Ian A.L. Getty and Antoine S. Lussier, 13–30. Vancouver: UBC Press, 1983.

Treaty Seven Tribal Council, Walter Hildebrandt, Dorothy First Rider, and Sarah Carter. *The True Spirit and Original Intent of Treaty 7.* Montreal: McGill-Queen's University Press, 1996.

Venne, Sharon. 'Understanding Treaty 6: An Indigenous Perspective.' In *Aboriginal and Treaty Rights in Canada: Essays on Law, Equality and Respect for Difference,* ed. Michael Asch, 173–207. Vancouver: University of British Columbia Press, 1997.

Walden, Keith. 'The Great March of the Mounted Police in Popular Literature, 1873–1973.' *Canadian Historical Association Historical Papers* (1980): 33–56.

Chapter 7   Ploughing Up the Middle Ground

Carter, Sarah. *Lost Harvests: Prairie Indian Reserve Farmers and Government Policy*. Montreal: McGill-Queen's University Press, 1990.

Dempsey, Hugh. *Big Bear: The End of Freedom*. Vancouver: Douglas and McIntyre, 1984.

Dyck, Noel. 'An Opportunity Lost: The Initiative of the Reserve Agricultural Programme in the Prairie West.' In *1885 and After: Native Society in Transition*, ed. F.L. Barron and James B. Waldram, 121–37. Regina: Canadian Plains Research Center, 1986.

Hunt, F.L. 'Notes on the Qu'Appelle Treaty.' *Canadian Monthly and National Review* 9/3 (1876).

Lux, Maureen. 'Beyond Biology: Disease and Its Impact on the Canadian Plains Native People.' Unpublished PhD diss., Simon Fraser University, 1996.

Tobias, John. 'Canada's Subjugation of the Plains Cree, 1879–1885.' *Canadian Historical Review* 64/4 (1983): 519–48.

Chapter 8   Turning Point: 1885 and After

Beal, Bob, and R.C. Macleod. *Prairie Fire: The 1885 North-West Rebellion*. Edmonton: Hurtig, 1984.

Bumsted, J.M. *The Peoples of Canada*, 2 vols. Toronto: Oxford University Press, 1992.

Carter, Sarah. *Capturing Women: The Manipulation of Cultural Imagery in Canada's Prairie West*. Montreal: McGill-Queen's University Press, 1997.

Flanagan, Thomas. *Louis Riel*. Canadian Historical Association Historical Booklet No. 50. Ottawa: Canadian Historical Association, 1992.

Fox, Uta H. 'The Failure of the Red Deer Industrial School.' Unpublished MA thesis, University of Calgary, 1993.

Hanson, S.D. '*Kitchi-manito-waya*.' In *Dictionary of Canadian Biography*, vol. 12: *1891–1900*. Toronto: University of Toronto Press, 1990.

Hildebrandt, Walter. *The Battle of Batoche: British Small Warfare and the Entrenched Metis.* Ottawa: National Historic Parks and Sites Branch, 1985.

– 'Official Images of 1885.' *Prairie Fire* 6/4 (1985): 31–8.

McCormack, Patricia A. 'Romancing the Northwest as Prescriptive History: Fort Chipewyan and the Northern Expansion of the Canadian State.' In *The Uncovered Past: Roots of Northern Alberta Societies,* ed. Patricia A. McCormack and R. Geoffrey Ironside, 89–104. Edmonton: Canadian Circumpolar Institute, 1993.

Miller, J.R. 'Owen Glendower, Hotspur and Canadian Indian Policy.' In *Sweet Promises: A Reader on Indian–White Relations in Canada,* ed. J.R. Miller, 323–52. Toronto: University of Toronto Press, 1991.

– *Shingwauk's Vision: A History of Native Residential Schools.* Toronto: University of Toronto Press, 1996.

Morton, Desmond. *The Last War Drum: The North-West Campaign of 1885.* Toronto: Hakkert, 1972.

Payment, Diane. *The Free People – Otipemisiwak: Batoche, Saskatchewan, 1870–1930.* Ottawa: Parks Canada, 1990.

Ray, Arthur J. 'The Northern Interior, 1600 to Modern Times.' In *The Cambridge History of the Native Peoples of the Americas,* vol. 2, eds. Bruce Trigger and Wilcomb E. Washburn, 259–328. Cambridge: Cambridge University Press, 1996.

Stonechild, Blair, and Bill Waiser. *Loyal till Death: Indians and the North-West Rebellion.* Calgary: Fifth House, 1997.

Titley, E. Brian. *A Narrow Vision: Duncan Campbell Scott and the Administration of Indian Affairs in Canada.* Vancouver: University of British Columbia Press, 1986.

Tough, Frank. *'As Their Natural Resources Fail': Native Peoples and the Economic History of Northern Manitoba, 1870–1930.* Vancouver: UBC Press, 1996.

Index

THEMES IN CANADIAN SOCIAL HISTORY

Editors:

Craig Heron 1997–
Franca Iacovetta 1997–1999